Fro

Welcome to our extra-s[...]astrological forecast which[...] up to the end of the centu[...] our year-ahead guides all th[...] tables and a calculator. Today,[...] ....ted .... to be made using ..ı computers, we have been able to build our knowledge and hard work into a program which calculates the precise astrological aspect for every day in a flash.

When Shakespeare wrote 'The fault, dear Brutus, is not in our stars, but in ourselves', he spoke for every astrologer. In our day-to-day forecasts we cannot hope to be 100% accurate every time, because this would remove the most important influence in your life, which is you! What we can hope to do is to give you a sense of the astrological backdrop to the day, week or month in question, and so prompt you to think a little harder about what is going in your own life, and thus help improve your chances of acting effectively to deal with events and situations.

During the course of a year, there may be one or two readings that are similar in nature. This is not an error, it is simply that the Moon or a planet has repeated a particular pattern. In addition, a planetary pattern that applies to your sign may apply to someone else's sign at some other point during the year. One planetary 'return' that you already know well is the Solar return that occurs every year on your birthday.

If you've read our guides before, you'll know that we're never less than positive and that our advice is unpretentious, down to earth, and rooted in daily experience. If this is the first time you've met us, please regard us not as in any way astrological gurus, but as good friends who wish you nothing but health, prosperity and contentment. Happy 1998-9!

Sasha Fenton is a world-renowned astrologer, palmist and Tarot card reader, with over 80 books published on Astrology, Palmistry, Tarot and other forms of divination. Now living in London, Sasha is a regular broadcaster on radio and television, as well as making frequent contributions to newspapers and magazines around the world, including South Africa and Australia. She is a former President and Secretary of the British Astrological and Psychic Society (BAPS) and Secretary of the Advisory Panel on Astrological Education.

Jonathan Dee is an astrologer, artist and historian based in Wales, and a direct descendant of the great Elizabethan alchemist and wizard Dr John Dee, court astrologer to Queen Elizabeth I. He has written a number of books, including the recently completed *The Chronicles of Ancient Egypt*, and for the last five years has co-written an annual astrological forecast series with Sasha Fenton. A regular broadcaster on television and radio, he has also hosted the Starline show for KQED Talk Radio, New Mexico.

YOUR DAY-BY-DAY FORECAST
SEPTEMBER 1998 – DECEMBER 1999

GEMINI

SASHA FENTON • JONATHAN DEE

HALDANE • MASON

Zambezi

DEDICATION

For the memory of Gary Bailey, a new star in heaven.

ACKNOWLEDGEMENTS

With many thanks to our computer wizard, Sean Lovatt.

———————————

This edition published 1998
by Haldane Mason Ltd
59 Chepstow Road
London W2 5BP

ISBN 1-902463-12-9

Designed and produced by Haldane Mason Ltd
Cover illustration by Lo Cole
Edited by Jan Budkowski

Printed in Singapore by Craft Print Pte Ltd

CONTENTS

An Astrological Overview of the 20th Century

Next year the shops will be full of astrology books for the new century and also for the new millennium. In this book, the last of the old century, we take a brief look back to see where the slow-moving outer planets were in each decade and what it meant. Obviously this will be no more than a very brief glance backwards but next year you will be able to see the picture in much more depth when we bring out our own book for the new millennium.

1900 - 1909

The century began with Pluto in Gemini and it was still in Gemini by the end of the decade. Neptune started out in Gemini but moved into cancer in 1901 and ended the decade still in Cancer. Uranus started the century in Sagittarius, moving to Capricorn in 1904 and ending the decade still in Capricorn. Saturn began the century in Sagittarius, moving to Capricorn in January 1900 and then through Aquarius, Pisces and Aries, ending the decade in Aries.

The stars and the decade

In general terms, the planet of upheaval in the dynastic sign of Sagittarius with Saturn also in that sign and Pluto opposing it, all at the very start of the century put the spotlight on dynasties, royalty and empires. As Saturn left for the 'establishment' sign of Capricorn these just about held together but as the decade ended, the power and control that these ancient dynasties had were loosening their grip on the developed world of the time. Queen Victoria died in 1901 and her son, Edward VII was dying by the end of the decade, so in Britain, the Victorian age of certainty was already coming to an end. The Boer War was only just won by Britain in 1902 which brought a shock to this successful colonial country.

Pluto in Gemini brought a transformation in methods of communications. It was as Saturn entered the innovative sign of Aquarius that these took concrete and useful form. Thus it was during this decade that the motor car, telephone, typewriter, gramophone and colour photography came into existence. Air travel began in 1900 with the first Zeppelin airship flight, the first powered aeroplane flight by the Wright brothers in 1904 and Louis Blériot's flight across the English Channel in 1909. Edison demonstrated the Kinetophone, the first machine capable of showing talking moving pictures in

1910. Even the nature of war changed as technologically modern Japan managed to fight off the might of the Russian empire in the war of 1904 - 1905.

The Treaty of Versailles, followed by further treaties of Aix and Trianon served to crush the German nation and therefore sow the seeds of the next war.

1910 – 1919

Pluto opened the decade in Gemini, moving to Cancer in 1913. Neptune travelled from Cancer to Leo in September 1914 while Uranus moved out of Capricorn, through Aquarius to end the decade in Pisces. Saturn moved from Aries to Taurus, then to Gemini, back into Taurus, then into Gemini again entering Cancer in 1914, then on through Leo and ending the decade in Virgo.

The stars and the decade

Now we see the start of a pattern. Sagittarius may be associated with dynasties but it is the home-loving and patriotic signs of Cancer and Leo that actually seem to be associated with major wars. The desire either to expand a country's domestic horizons or to protect them from the expansion of others is ruled by the maternal sign of Cancer, followed by the paternal one of Leo. Home, family, tradition, safety all seem to be fought over when major planets move through these signs. When future generations learn about the major wars of the 20th century they will probably be lumped together in their minds - despite the 20-year gap between them - just as we lump the Napoleonic wars together, forgetting that there was a nine-year gap between them, and of course, this long stay of Pluto in Cancer covered the whole of this period.

It is interesting to note that Pluto moved into Cancer in July 1913 and Neptune entered Leo on the 23rd of September 1914, just three of weeks after the outbreak of the First World War. Saturn moved into Cancer in April 1914. Pluto is associated with transformation, Neptune with dissolution and Saturn with loss, sadness and sickness. Many people suffered and so many families and dynasties were unexpectedly dissolved at that time, among these, the Romanov Czar and his family and the kings of Portugal, Hungary, Italy and Germany and the Manchu dynasty of China. America (born on the 4th of July, 1776 and therefore a Cancerian country) was thrust into prominence as a major economic and social power after this war. Russia experienced the Bolshevik revolution during it. As Saturn moved into Virgo (the sign that is associated with health) at the end of this decade, a world-wide plague of influenza killed 20 million people, far more than had died during the course of the war itself.

1920 – 1929

The roaring 20s began and ended with Pluto in Cancer. Neptune moved from Leo to Virgo at the end of this decade and Uranus moved from Pisces to Aries in 1927. Saturn travelled from Virgo, through Libra, Scorpio, Sagittarius and then backwards and forwards between Sagittarius and Capricorn, ending up in Capricorn at the end of 1929.

The stars and the decade

Pluto's long transformative reign in Cancer made life hard for men during this time. Cancer is the most female of all the signs, being associated with nurturing and motherhood. Many men were sick in mind and body as a result of the war and women began to take proper jobs for the first time. Family planning and better living conditions brought improvements in life for ordinary people and in the developed world there was a major boom in house building as well as in improved road and rail commuter systems. The time of lords and ladies was passing and ordinary people were demanding better conditions. Strikes and unrest were common, especially in Germany. As the decade ended, the situation both domestically and in the foreign policies of the developed countries began to look up. Even the underdeveloped countries began to modernize a little. Shortly before the middle of this decade, all the politicians who might have prevented the rise of Hitler and the Nazi party died and then came the stock market crash of 1929. The probable astrological sequence that set this train of circumstances off was the run up to the opposition of Saturn in Capricorn to Pluto in Cancer which took place in 1931. The effects of such major planetary events are often felt while the planets are closing into a conjunction or opposition etc., rather than just at the time of their exactitude.

On a brighter note great strides were made in the worlds of art, music and film and ordinary people could enjoy more entertainment than ever before, in 1929 the first colour television was demonstrated and in 1928 Alexander Fleming announced his discovery of penicillin. At the very start of the decade prohibition passed into US Federal law, ushering in the age of organized crime and as a spin-off a great increase in drinking in that country and later on, all those wonderful gangster films. The same year, the partition of Ireland took place bringing more conflict and this time on a very long-term basis.

1930 – 1939

The 1930s should have been better than the 1920s but they were not. Pluto remained in Cancer until 1937, Neptune remained in Virgo throughout the decade, Uranus entered Taurus in 1934 and Saturn moved from Capricorn through Aquarius, Pisces then back and forth between Aries and Pisces, ending the decade in Taurus.

The stars and the decade

Neptune's voyage through Virgo did help in the field of advances in medicine and in public health. Pluto continued to make life hard for men and then by extension for families, while in the 'motherhood' sign of Cancer. While Saturn was in the governmental signs of Capricorn and Aquarius, democracy ceased to exist anywhere in the world. In the UK a coalition government was in power for most of the decade while in the USA, Franklin Delano Roosevelt ruled as a kind of benign emperor for almost three terms of office, temporarily dismantling much of that country's democratic machinery while he did so. Governments in Russia, Germany, Italy, Spain and Japan moved to dictatorships or dictatorial types of government with all the resultant tyranny, while France, Britain and even the USA floundered for much of the time. China was ruled by warring factions. However, there was an upsurge of popular entertainment at this time, especially through the mediums of film, music and radio probably due to the advent of adventurous, inventive Uranus into the music and entertainment sign of Taurus in 1934.

1940 – 1949

War years once again. Pluto remained in the 'paternal' sign of Leo throughout this decade, bringing tyranny and control of the masses in all the developed countries and also much of the Third World. Neptune entered Libra in 1942, Uranus moved from Taurus to Gemini in 1941, then to Cancer in 1948. Saturn began the decade in Taurus, moved to Gemini, Cancer, Leo and finally Virgo during this decade. The 'home and country' signs of Cancer and Leo were once more thrust into the limelight in a war context. Neptune is not a particularly warlike planet and Libra is normally a peaceable sign but Libra does rule open enemies as well as peace and harmony.

The stars and the decade

To continue looking for the moment at the planet Neptune, astrologers don't take its dangerous side seriously enough. Neptune can use the sea in a particularly destructive manner when it wants to with tidal waves, disasters at sea and so on, so it is interesting to note that the war in the West was almost lost for the allies at sea due to the success of the German U-boats. Hitler gambled on a quick end to the war in the east and shut his mind to Napoleon's experience of the Russian winter. Saturn through Cancer and Leo, followed by the inventive sign of Uranus entering Cancer at the end of the decade almost brought home, family, tradition and the world itself to an end with the explosions of the first atomic bombs.

However, towards the end of this decade, it became clear that democracy, the rights of ordinary people and a better lifestyle for everybody were a better answer than trying to find 'lebensraum' by pinching one's neighbour's land and enslaving its population. Saturn's entry into Virgo brought great advances in medicine and the plagues and diseases of the past began to diminish throughout the world. Pluto in Leo transformed the power structures of every country and brought such ideas as universal education, better housing and social security systems - at least in the developed world.

1950 - 1959

Pluto still dipped in and out of Leo until it finally left for Virgo in 1957. Neptune finally left Libra for Scorpio in 1955, Uranus sat on that dangerous and warlike cusp of Cancer and Leo, while Saturn moved swiftly through Virgo, Libra, Scorpio, Sagittarius and then into Capricorn.

The stars and the decade

The confrontations between dictators and between dictatorships and democracy continued during this time with the emphasis shifting to the conflict between communism and capitalism. The Korean war started the decade and the communist take-over in China ended it. Military alertness was reflected in the UK by the two years of national service that young men were obliged to perform throughout the decade. Rationing, shortages of food, fuel and consumer goods remained in place for half the decade, but by the end of it, the world was becoming a very different place. With American money, Germany and Japan were slowly rebuilt, communism did at least bring a measure of stability in China and the Soviet Union, although its pervasive power brought fear and peculiar witch hunts in the United States. In Europe and the USA the lives of ordinary people improved beyond belief.

Pluto in Virgo brought plenty of work for the masses and for ordinary people, poverty began to recede for the first time in history. Better homes, labour-saving devices and the vast amount of popular entertainment in the cinema, the arts, popular music and television at long last brought fun into the lives of most ordinary folk. In Britain and the Commonwealth, in June 1953, the coronation of the new Queen ushered in a far more optimistic age while her Empire dissolved around her.

GEMINI

1960 - 1969

This is the decade that today's middle-aged folk look back on with fond memories, yet it was not always as safe as we like to think. Pluto remained in Virgo throughout the decade bringing work and better health to many people. Neptune remained in Scorpio throughout this time, while Uranus traversed back and forth between Leo and Virgo, then from Virgo to Libra, ending the decade in Libra. Saturn hovered around the cusp of Taurus and Gemini until the middle of the decade and then on through Gemini and Cancer, spending time around the Cancer/Leo cusp and then on through Leo to rest once again on the Leo/Virgo cusp.

The stars and the decade

The Cancer/Leo threats of atomic war were very real in the early 1960s, with the Cuban missile crisis bringing America and the Soviet Union to the point of war. The Berlin wall went up. President Kennedy's assassination in November 1963 shocked the world and the atmosphere of secrets, spies and mistrust abounded in Europe, the USA and in the Soviet Union. One of the better manifestations of this time of cold war, CIA dirty tricks and spies was the plethora of wonderful spy films and television programmes of the early 60s. Another was the sheer fun of the Profumo affair!

The late 1960s brought the start of a very different atmosphere. The Vietnam War began to be challenged by the teenagers whose job it was to die in it and the might of America was severely challenged by these tiny Vietcong soldiers in black pyjamas and sandals. The wave of materialism of the 1950s was less attractive to the flower-power generation of the late 60s. The revolutionary planet Uranus in balanced Libra brought the protest movement into being and an eventual end to racial segregation in the USA. Equality between the sexes was beginning to be considered. The troubles of Northern Ireland began at the end of this decade.

In 1969, Neil Armstrong stepped out onto the surface of the Moon, thereby marking the start of a very different age, the New Age, the Age of Aquarius.

1970 - 1979

Pluto began the decade around the Virgo/Libra cusp, settling in Libra in 1972 and remaining there for the rest of the decade. Neptune started the decade by moving back and forth between Scorpio and Sagittarius and residing in Sagittarius for the rest of the decade. Uranus hovered between Libra and Scorpio until 1975 and then travelled through Scorpio until the end of the decade while Saturn moved from Taurus to Gemini, then hung around the Cancer/Leo cusp and finally moved into Virgo.

The stars and the decade

The planets in or around that dangerous Cancer/Leo cusp and the continuing Libran emphasis brought more danger from total war as America struggled with Vietnam and the cold war. However, the influence of Virgo brought work, an easier life and more hope than ever to ordinary people in the First World. Uranus in Libra brought different kinds of love partnerships into public eye as fewer people bothered to marry. Divorce became easier and homosexuality became legal. With Uranus opening the doors to secretive Scorpio, spies such as Burgess, Maclean, Philby, Lonsdale and Penkowski began to come in from the cold. President Nixon was nicely caught out at Watergate, ushering in a time of more openness in governments everywhere.

If you are reading this book, you may be doing so because you are keen to know about yourself and your sign, but you are likely to be quite interested in astrology and perhaps in other esoteric techniques. You can thank the atmosphere of the 1970s for the openness and the lack of fear and superstition which these subjects now enjoy. The first festival of Mind, Body and Spirit took place in 1976 and the British Astrological and Psychic Society was launched in the same year, both of these events being part of the increasing interest in personal awareness and alternative lifestyles.

Neptune in Scorpio brought fuel crises and Saturn through Cancer and Leo brought much of the repression of women to an end, with some emancipation from tax and social anomalies. Tea bags and instant coffee allowed men for the first time to cope with the terrible hardship of making a cuppa!

1980 - 1989

Late in 1983, Pluto popped into the sign of Scorpio, popped out again and re-entered it in 1984. Astrologers of the 60s and 70s feared this planetary situation in case it brought the ultimate Plutonic destruction with it. Instead of this, the Soviet Union and South Africa freed themselves from tyranny and the Berlin Wall came down. The main legacy of Pluto in Scorpio is the Scorpionic association of danger through sex, hence the rise of AIDS. Neptune began the decade in Sagittarius then it travelled back and forth over the Sagittarius/Capricorn cusp, ending the decade in Capricorn. Uranus moved from Scorpio, back and forth over the Scorpio/Sagittarius cusp, then through Sagittarius, ending the decade in Capricorn. Saturn began the decade in Virgo, then hovered around the Virgo/Libra cusp, through Libra, Scorpio and Sagittarius, resting along the Sagittarius/Capricorn cusp, ending the decade in Capricorn.

The stars and the decade

The movement of planets through the dynastic sign of Sagittarius brought doubt and uncertainty to Britain's royal family, while the planets in authoritative Capricorn brought strong government to the UK in the form of Margaret Thatcher. Ordinary people began to seriously question the *status quo* and to attempt to change it. Even in the hidden empire of China, modernization and change began to creep in. Britain went to war again by sending the gunboats to the Falkland Islands to fight off a truly old-fashioned takeover bid by the daft Argentinean dictator, General Galtieri.

Saturn is an earth planet, Neptune rules the sea, while Uranus is associated with the air. None of these planets was in their own element and this may have had something to do with the increasing number of natural and man-made disasters that disrupted the surface of the earth during this decade. The first space shuttle flight took place in 1981 and the remainder of the decade reflected many people's interest in extra-terrestrial life in the form of films and television programmes. ET went home. Black rap music and the casual use of drugs became a normal part of the youth scene. Maybe the movement of escapist Neptune through the 'outer space' sign of Sagittarius had something to do with this.

1990 – 1999

Pluto began the decade in Scorpio, moving in and out of Sagittarius until 1995 remaining there for the rest of the decade. Neptune began the decade in Capricorn, travelling back and forth over the cusp of Aquarius, ending the decade in Aquarius, Uranus moved in and out of Aquarius, remaining there from 1996 onwards. Saturn travelled from Capricorn, through Aquarius, Pisces (and back again), then on through Pisces, Aries, in and out of Taurus, finally ending the decade in Taurus.

The stars and the decade

The Aquarian emphasis has brought advances in science and technology and a time when computers are common even in the depths of darkest Africa. The logic and fairness of Aquarius does seem to have affected many of the peoples of the earth. Pluto in the open sign of Sagittarius brought much governmental secrecy to an end, it will also transform the traditional dynasties of many countries before it leaves them for good. The aftermath of the dreadful and tragic death of Princess Diana in 1997 put a rocket under the creaking 19th-century habits of British royalty.

The final decade began with yet another war – this time the Gulf War – which sent a serious signal to all those who fancy trying their hand at international bullying or the 19th-century tactics of pinching your neighbour's land and resources. Uranus's last fling in Capricorn tore up the earth with volcanoes and earthquakes, and its stay in Aquarius seems to be keeping this pattern going. Saturn in Pisces, opposite the 'health' sign of Virgo is happily bringing new killer viruses into being and encouraging old ones to build up resistance to antibiotics. The bubonic plague is alive and well in tropical countries along with plenty of other plagues that either are, or are becoming resistant to modern medicines. Oddly enough the planetary line-up in 1997 was similar to that of the time of the great plague of London in 1665!

Films, the arts, architecture all showed signs of beginning an exciting period of revolution in 1998. Life became more electronic and computer-based for the younger generation while in the old world, the vast army of the elderly began to struggle with a far less certain world of old-age poverty and strange and frightening innovations. Keeping up to date and learning to adapt is the only way to survive now, even for the old folks.

It is interesting to note that the first event of importance to shock Europe in this century was the morganatic marriage of Franz Ferdinand, the heir to the massively powerful Austro-Hungarian throne. This took place in the summer of 1900. The unpopularity of this controlling and repressive empire fell on its head in Sarajevo on the 28th of July 1914. This mighty empire is now almost forgotten, but its death throes are still being played out in and around Sarajevo today - which only goes to show how long it can take for anything to be settled.

Technically the twentieth century only ends at the beginning of the year 2001 but most of us will be celebrating the end of the century and the end of the millennium and the end of the last day of 1999 - that is if we are all here of course! A famous prediction of global disaster comes from the writings of the French writer, doctor and astrologer Nostradamus (1503–66):

- The year 1999, seventh month,
- From the sky will come a great King of Terror:
- To bring back to life the great King of the Mongols,
- Before and after Mars reigns.
  (Quatrain X:72 from the *Centuries*)

Jonathan has worked out that with the adjustments of the calendar from the time of Nostradamus, the date of the predicted disaster will be the 11th of August 1999. As it happens there will be a total eclipse of the Sun at ten past eleven on that day at 18 degrees of Leo. We have already seen how the signs of Cancer, Leo and Libra seem to be the ones that are most clearly associated with war and this reference to 'Mars reigning' is the fact that Mars is the god of war. Therefore, the prediction suggests that an Oriental king will wage a war from the sky that brings terror to the world. Some people have suggested that this event would bring about the end of the world but that is not what the prediction actually says. A look back over the 1900s has proved this whole century to be one of terror from the skies but it would be awful to think that there would be yet another war, this time emanating from Mongolia. Terrible but not altogether impossible to imagine I guess. Well, let us hope that we are all here for us to write and for you to enjoy the next set of zodiac books for the turn of the millennium and beyond.

2000 onwards: a very brief look forward

The scientific exploration and eventual colonization of space is on the way now. Scorpio rules fossil fuels and there will be no major planets passing through this sign for quite a while so alternative fuel sources will have to be sought. Maybe it will be the entry of Uranus into the pioneering sign of Aries in January 2012 that will make a start on this. The unusual line up of the 'ancient seven' planets of Sun, Moon, Mercury, Venus, Mars and Saturn in Taurus on the 5th of May 2000 will be interesting. Taurus represents such matters as land, farming, building, cooking, flowers, the sensual beauty of music, dancing and the arts. Jonathan and Sasha will work out the astrological possibilities for the future in depth and put out ideas together for you in a future book.

The Essential Gemini

YOUR RULING PLANET Your ruling body is Mercury, the Roman god who was the swift-witted messenger of the gods. His principal job was to do Jupiter's dirty work for him.

YOUR SYMBOL Your symbol is the Twins, which are in this case the heavenly twins, Castor and Pollux. The symbol of the heavenly twins is known in many cultures, including the Red Indian one. The Bible emphasizes the rivalry of twins in the story of Cain and Abel.

PARTS OF THE BODY The upper respiratory system, the shoulders, arms, wrists and hands. Gemini also rules the nervous system and the mind so any kind of nervous ailment can be expected, especially skin problems.

YOUR GOOD BITS Mental agility, adaptability, the ability to communicate and a sense of humour.

YOUR BAD BITS Lack of sympathy when others are ill or unhappy. Selfishness and self-absorption. Hopping from one idea to another. Telling lies when it suits you.

YOUR WEAKNESSES Chatting on the phone for hours. Smoking (a high proportion of Geminis smoke. Those who don't make a great fuss about cigarette smoke which inevitably drifts across the room to them).

YOUR BEST DAY Wednesday, because it is associated with the Roman god, Mercury.

YOUR WORST DAY Friday.

YOUR COLOURS Yellow, black-and-white check and multicoloured mixtures.

CITIES London, Bruges, San Francisco, Melbourne.

COUNTRIES Wales, Japan, Indonesia.

HOLIDAYS You enjoy a good old-fashioned beach holiday where you can soak up the sun. You enjoy any place that has a variety of shops and interesting places to eat out in and also plenty to see.

YOUR FAVOURITE CAR A small, fast sports car. Even if you have absolutely no money at all, you need to be mobile and, therefore, you will put up with any kind of broken-down transport rather than to be without wheels.

YOUR FAVOURITE MEAL OUT Question: what does the Gemini make for dinner? Answer: reservations! You prefer light and tasty dishes or simple foods like fish and chips or salads to overcooked dishes or piles of unidentified mush. Many Geminis enjoy Chinese food because it consists of tasty titbits. Many of you are vegetarians. We are tempted to say that your favourite foods are a glass of wine, a cup of coffee, a cigarette and a few vitamin pills, because many Geminis are not really into eating – indeed, most of you are happy with a drink and a cigarette and the occasional tomato sandwich to keep you from keeling over. Tradition ascribes beans to your sign.

YOUR FAVOURITE DRINK This is quite an addictive sign and a great many Geminis drink heavily. Whether a light or a heavy drinker, most seem to enjoy spirits of all kinds and either wine, beer or lager with a meal. Cocktails and mixed drinks are liked too.

YOUR HERBS Marjoram.

YOUR TREES Nut trees, especially the walnut.

YOUR FLOWERS Lily of the valley, lavender, orchid and the gladiolus.

YOUR ANIMALS Hyena, monkey, parrot, stork.

YOUR METAL Mercury.

YOUR GEMS There are various gems associated with your sign, including the agate, alexandrite and onyx.

MODE OF DRESS Anything which allows you to move around quickly and which is in the latest fashion. High-fashion sports clothes are ideal. You love clothes and will spend a lot of money on good ones.

YOUR CAREERS Anything which involves communication. Thus, writer, journalist, teacher, telephonist, salesperson, taxi driver, courier, travel agent, cabin crew on an aircraft, pilot.

YOUR FRIENDS Must be intelligent, humorous, interesting people.

YOUR ENEMIES Dull, mean or crabby types. Quiet or introverted people or spiteful and offensive ones.

YOUR FAVOURITE GIFT Stationery makes a good stocking-filler for you while a good-quality pen and pencil set or a maths set would suit some of you. Airline tickets to a hot place would delight you as would a hands-on day at a race track. You love books, computer equipment, cellphones, and electronic address books. Also anything in a clever box or bag such as make-up, bathroom stuff and a manicure set.

YOUR IDEAL HOME A home where the air is fresh and with room for a garden. Plenty of storage space for your collection of gadgets and at least three telephones! You also need a maid to do the cleaning and ironing for you and someone to clean up the mess that your animals leave.

YOUR FAVOURITE BOOKS Autobiographies, psychology and astrology books.

YOUR FAVOURITE MUSIC Anything with clever, meaningful lyrics and compilations.

YOUR GAMES AND SPORTS Badminton, tennis, word games, board games.

YOUR PAST AND FUTURE LIVES There are many theories about past lives and even some about future ones but the one we are suggesting in this book is that your immediate past life was ruled by the previous sign to yours and that your future one will be governed by the following sign to yours. Thus, in your case, you will have been a Taurean in your previous life and you will be a Cancerian in the next one. If you want to know all about either of these signs, zip straight out to the shops and buy our books on them. Jonathan Dee and Sasha Fenton are both born under signs that just love to sell lots of books!

YOUR LUCKY NUMBER Your lucky number is 3. To find your lucky number on a raffle ticket or something similar, first add the numbers together. For example, if one of your lottery numbers is 28, add 2 + 8 to make 10; then add 1 + 0, to give the root number of 1. The number 316 on a raffle ticket works in the same way. Add 3 + 1 + 6 to make 10: then add 1 + 0, making 1. As your lucky number is 3, anything that adds up to this, such as 21, 147 or 30 would do nicely. A selection of lottery numbers should include some of the following: 3, 12, 30, 39 or 48.

Your Sun Sign

Your Sun Sign is determined by your date of birth.
Thus anyone born between 21st March and 20th April is Aries and so
on through the calendar. Your Rising Sign (see page 36)
is determined by the day and time of your birth.

GEMINI

RULED BY MERCURY
21st May – 21st June

Yours is a masculine, air sign and your symbol is the twins. This makes you restless, adventurous, outgoing, curious and, sometimes, a nervous wreck.

You do six things at once while chatting on the phone at the same time, you are easily bored and variety is the spice of your life. You need a job which is different from one day to another and you try to get the more mundane chores out of the way quickly. You have a reputation for knowing a little about a lot of things but this is unfair and untrue. The chances are that you have a good deal of knowledge of at least one important subject but you are interested in everything that is going on around you. Your curiosity leads you to find out about a great many things and you constantly try out new ideas on your friends and family. Geminis of both sexes like to live in neat and orderly surroundings but you are not keen on doing the housework yourself. If you are wise, you will choose a partner who will take some of the cooking and cleaning off your hands. You enjoy being with young people because you tend to stay young yourself throughout life. Some of you teach, or work with the young as a hobby.

You have a reputation for flirtatiousness but this is also somewhat unfounded. You love to chat to members of the opposite sex and you thoroughly enjoy parties and social occasions which allow you to mix with all kinds of people and ask them about their lives. Geminis make excellent journalists, partly due to your natural curiosity and partly due to your ability to write, talk and communicate ideas to others.

In permanent relationships, you are actually very faithful, partly because you fear abandonment yourself and therefore, would never allow a partner to feel insecure if you can help it. You remain close to your children and you take an intelligent interest in their lives. You can try to interfere on occasion.

Some Geminis spend money like water, especially on clothes, eating out and travelling, but you tend to earn this money yourself rather than demanding it from your partner. Most of you are generous, but you hate being taken for a fool or lending money which is not repaid. You need trust and freedom in a relationship and you respect a partner's need for independence. You may miss out on the joys of childhood, possibly because your parents were selfish or difficult, or for reasons beyond anyone's control. The chances are that you didn't get on well with your brothers and sisters or that you had a hard time at school. This leaves you with a need for a close and loving family of your own and you may marry early in order to find this. If your marriage doesn't work you will eventually try to find someone else.

You are probably quite a clever business person, finding ingenious ways of making or saving money for yourself and the people you work for. You prefer to work near telephones, fax machines and among people because communication interests you. Many of you make excellent accountants. Having said that, you are clever with your hands and may be keen on mending cars, making small items or knitting. Your nerves are your greatest enemy and many of you are heavy smokers, relying on nicotine to calm you down when the going gets rough. You love to work and to socialize and many of you are great travellers. You are not a split personality or two-faced in any way, but you have many talents and also different friends to suit your different moods.

All the Other Sun Signs

ARIES
21st March to 20th April

Ariens can get anything they want off the ground, but they may land back down again with a bump. Quick to think and to act, Ariens are often intelligent and have little patience with fools. This includes anyone who is slower than themselves.

They are not the tidiest of people and they are impatient with details, except when engaged upon their special subject; then Ariens can fiddle around for hours. They are willing to make huge financial sacrifices for their families and they can put up with relatives living with them as long as this leaves them free to do their own thing. Aries women are decisive and competitive at work but many are disinterested in homemaking. They might consider giving up a relationship if it interfered with their ambitions. Highly sexed and experimental, they are faithful while in love but, if love begins to fade, they start to look around. Ariens may tell themselves that they are only looking for amusement, but they may end up in a fulfilling relationship with someone else's partner. This kind of situation offers the continuity and emotional support which they need with no danger of boredom or entrapment.

Their faults are those of impatience and impetuosity, coupled with a hot temper. They can pick a furious row with a supposed adversary, tear him or her to pieces then walk away from the situation five minutes later, forgetting all about it. Unfortunately, the poor victim can't always shake off the effects of the row in quite the same way. However, Arien cheerfulness, spontaneous generosity and kindness make them the greatest friends to have.

TAURUS
21st April to 21st May

These people are practical and persevering. Taureans are solid and reliable, regular in habits, sometimes a bit wet behind the ears and stubborn as mules. Their love of money and the comfort it can bring may make them very materialistic in outlook. They are most suited to a practical career which brings with it few surprises and plenty of money. However, they have a strong artistic streak which can be expressed in work, hobbies and interests.

Some Taureans are quick and clever, highly amusing and quite outrageous in appearance, but underneath this crazy exterior is a background of true talent and very hard work. This type may be a touch arrogant. Other Taureans hate to be rushed or hassled, preferring to work quietly and thoroughly at their own pace. They take relationships very seriously and make safe and reliable partners. They may keep their worries to themselves but they are not usually liars or sexually untrustworthy.

Being so very sensual as well as patient, these people make excellent lovers. Their biggest downfall comes later in life when they have a tendency to plonk themselves down in front of the television night after night, tuning out the rest of the world. Another problem with some Taureans is their 'pet hate', which they'll harp on about at any given opportunity. Their virtues are common sense, loyalty, responsibility and a pleasant, non-hostile approach to others. Taureans are much brighter than anyone gives them credit, and it is hard to beat them in an argument because they usually know what they are talking about. If a Taurean is on your side, they make wonderful friends and comfortable and capable colleagues.

CANCER
22nd June to 23rd July

Cancerians look for security on the one hand and adventure and novelty on the other. They are popular because they really listen to what others are saying. Their own voices are attractive too. They are naturals for sales work and in any kind of advisory capacity. Where their own problems are concerned, they can disappear inside themselves and brood, which makes it hard for others to understand them. Cancerians spend a good deal of time worrying about their families and, even more so, about money. They appear soft but are very hard to influence.

Many Cancerians are small traders and many more work in teaching or the caring professions. They have a feel for history, perhaps collecting historical mementoes, and their memories are excellent. They need to have a home but they love to travel away from it, being happy in the knowledge that it is there waiting for them to come back to. There are a few Cancerians who seem to drift through life and expect other members of their family to keep them.

Romantically, they prefer to be settled and they fear being alone. A marriage would need to be really bad before they consider leaving, and if they do, they soon look for a new partner. These people can be scoundrels in business because they hate parting with money once they have their hands on it. However, their charm and intelligence usually manage to get them out of trouble.

LEO
24th July to 23rd August

Leos can be marvellous company or a complete pain in the neck. Under normal circumstances, they are warm-hearted, generous, sociable and popular but they can be very moody and irritable when under pressure or under the weather. Leos put their heart and soul into whatever they are doing and they can work like demons for a while. However, they cannot keep up the pace for long and they need to get away, zonk out on the sofa and take frequent holidays. These people always appear confident and they look like true winners, but their confidence can suddenly evaporate, leaving them unsure and unhappy with their efforts. They are extremely sensitive to hurt and they cannot take ridicule or even very much teasing.

Leos are proud. They have very high standards in all that they do and most have great integrity and honesty, but there are some who are complete and utter crooks. These people can stand on their dignity and be very snobbish.

Their arrogance can become insufferable and they can take their powers of leadership into the realms of bossiness. They are convinced that they should be in charge and they can be very obstinate. Some Leos love the status and lifestyle which proclaims their successes. Many work in glamour professions such as the airline and entertainment industries. Others spend their day communing with computers and other high-tech gadgetry. In loving relationships, they are loyal but only while the magic lasts. If boredom sets in, they often start looking around for fresh fields. They are the most generous and loving of people and they need to play affectionately. Leos are kind, charming and they live life to the full.

VIRGO
24th August to 23rd September

Virgos are highly intelligent, interested in everything and everyone and happy to be busy with many jobs and hobbies. Many have some kind of specialized knowledge and most are good with their hands, but their nit-picking ways can infuriate colleagues. They find it hard to discuss their innermost feelings and this can make them hard to understand. In many ways, they are happier doing something practical than dealing with relationships. Virgos can also overdo the self-sacrificial bit and make themselves martyrs to other people's impractical lifestyles. They are willing to fit in with whatever is going on and can adjust to most things, but they mustn't neglect their own needs.

Although excellent communicators and wonderfully witty conversationalists, Virgos prefer to express their deepest feelings by actions rather than words. Most avoid touching all but very close friends and family members and many find lovey-dovey behaviour embarrassing. They can be very highly sexed and may use this as a way of expressing love. Virgos are criticized a good deal as children and are often made to feel unwelcome in their childhood homes. In turn, they become very critical of others and they can use this in order to wound.

Many Virgos overcome inhibitions by taking up acting, music, cookery or sports. Acting is particularly common to this sign because it allows them to put aside their fears and take on the mantle of someone quite different. They are shy and slow to make friends but when they do accept someone, they are the loyalest, gentlest and kindest of companions. They are great company and have a wonderful sense of humour.

LIBRA
24th September to 23rd October

Librans have a deceptive appearance, looking soft but being tough and quite selfish underneath. Astrological tradition tells us that this sign is dedicated to marriage, but a high proportion of them prefer to remain single, particularly when a difficult relationship comes to an end. These people are great to tell secrets to because they never listen to anything properly and promptly forget whatever is said. The confusion between their desire to co-operate with others and the need for self-expression is even more evident when at work. The best job is one where they are a part of an organization but able to take responsibility and make their own decisions.

While some Librans are shy and lacking in confidence, others are strong and determined with definite leadership qualities. All need to find a job that entails dealing with others and which does not wear out their delicate nerves. All Librans are charming, sophisticated and diplomatic, but can be confusing for others. All have a strong sense of justice and fair play but most haven't the strength to take on a determinedly lame duck. They project an image which is attractive, chosen to represent their sense of status and refinement. Being inclined to experiment sexually, they are not the most faithful of partners and even goody-goody Librans are terrible flirts.

SCORPIO
24th October to 22nd November

Reliable, resourceful and enduring, Scorpios seem to be the strong men and women of the zodiac. But are they really? They can be nasty at times, dishing out what they see as the truth, no matter how unwelcome. Their own feelings are sensitive and they are easily hurt, but they won't show any hurt or weakness in themselves to others. When they are very low or unhappy, this turns inwards, attacking their immune systems and making them ill. However, they have great resilience and they bounce back time and again from the most awful ailments.

Nobody needs to love and be loved more than a Scorpio, but their partners must stand up to them because they will give anyone they don't respect a very hard time indeed. They are the most loyal and honest of companions, both in personal relationships and at work. One reason for this is their hatred of change or uncertainty. Scorpios enjoy being the power behind the throne with someone else occupying the hot seat. This way, they can quietly manipulate everyone, set one against another and get exactly what they want from the situation.

Scorpios' voices are their best feature, often low, well-modulated and cultured and these wonderful voices are used to the full in pleasant persuasion. These people are neither as highly sexed nor as difficult as most astrology books make out, but they do have their passions (even if these are not always for sex itself) and they like to be thought of as sexy. They love to shock and to appear slightly dangerous, but they also make kind-hearted and loyal friends, superb hosts and gentle people who are often very fond of animals. Great people when they are not being cruel, stingy or devious!

SAGITTARIUS
23rd November to 21st December

Sagittarians are great company because they are interested in everything and everyone. Broad-minded and lacking in prejudice, they are fascinated by even the strangest of people. With their optimism and humour, they are often the life and soul of the party, while they are in a good mood. They can become quite down-hearted, crabby and awkward on occasion, but not usually for long. They can be hurtful to others because they cannot resist speaking what they see as the truth, even if it causes embarrassment. However, their tactlessness is usually innocent and they have no desire to hurt.

Sagittarians need an unconventional lifestyle, preferably one which allows them to travel. They cannot be cooped up in a cramped environment and they need to meet new people and to explore a variety of ideas during their day's work. Money is not their god and they will work for a pittance if they feel inspired by the task. Their values are spiritual rather than material. Many are attracted to the spiritual side of life and may be interested in the Church, philosophy, astrology and other New Age subjects. Higher education and legal matters attract them because these subjects expand and explore intellectual boundaries. Long-lived relationships may not appeal because they need to feel free and unfettered, but they can do well with a self-sufficient and independent partner. Despite all this intellectualism and need for freedom, Sagittarians have a deep need to be cuddled and touched and they need to be supported emotionally.

CAPRICORN
22nd December to 20th January

Capricorns are patient, realistic and responsible and they take life seriously. They need security but they may find this difficult to achieve. Many live on a treadmill of work, simply to pay the bills and feed the kids. They will never shun family responsibilities, even caring for distant relatives if this becomes necessary. However, they can play the martyr while doing so. These people hate coarseness, they are easily embarrassed and they hate to annoy anyone. Capricorns believe fervently in keeping the peace in their families. This doesn't mean that they cannot stand up for themselves, indeed they know how to get their own way and they won't be bullied. They are adept at using charm to get around prickly people.

Capricorns are ambitious, hard-working, patient and status-conscious and they will work their way steadily towards the top in any organization. If they run their own businesses, they need a partner with more pizzazz to deal with sales and marketing for them while they keep an eye on the books. Their nit-picking habits can infuriate others and some have a tendency to 'know best' and not to listen. These people work at their hobbies with the same kind of dedication that they put into everything else. They are faithful and reliable in relationships and it takes a great deal to make them stray. If a relationship breaks up, they take a long time to get over it. They may marry very early or delay it until middle age when they are less shy. As an earth sign, Capricorns are highly sexed but they need to be in a relationship where they can relax and gain confidence. Their best attribute is their genuine kindness and their wonderfully dry, witty sense of humour.

AQUARIUS
21st January to 19th February

Clever, friendly, kind and humane, Aquarians are the easiest people to make friends with but probably the hardest to really know. They are often more comfortable with acquaintances than with those who are close to them. Being dutiful, they would never let a member of their family go without their basic requirements, but they can be strangely, even deliberately, blind to their underlying needs and real feelings. They are more comfortable with causes and their idealistic ideas than with the day-to-day routine of family life. Their homes may reflect this lack of interest by being rather messy, although there are other Aquarians who are almost clinically house proud.

Their opinions are formed early in life and are firmly fixed. Being patient with people, they make good teachers and are, themselves, always willing to learn something new. But are they willing to go out and earn a living? Some are, many are not. These people can be extremely eccentric in the way they dress or the way they live. They make a point of being 'different' and they can actually feel very unsettled and uneasy if made to conform, even outwardly. Their restless, sceptical minds mean that they need an alternative kind of lifestyle which stretches them mentally.

In relationships, they are surprisingly constant and faithful and they only stray when they know in their hearts that there is no longer anything to be gained from staying put. Aquarians are often very attached to the first real commitment in their lives and they can even remarry a previously divorced partner. Their sexuality fluctuates, perhaps peaking for some years then pushed aside while something else occupies their energies, then high again. Many Aquarians are extremely highly sexed and very clever and active in bed.

PISCES
20th February to 20th March

This idealistic, dreamy, kind and impractical sign needs a lot of understanding. They have a fractured personality which has so many sides and so many moods that they probably don't even understand themselves. Nobody is more kind, thoughtful and caring, but they have a tendency to drift away from people and responsibilities. When the going gets rough, they get going! Being creative, clever and resourceful, these people can achieve a great deal and really reach the top, but few of them do. Some Pisceans have a self-destruct button which they press before reaching their goal. Others do achieve success and the motivating force behind this essentially spiritual and mystical sign is often money. Many Pisceans feel insecure, most suffer some experience of poverty at some time in their early lives and they grow into adulthood determined that they will never feel that kind of uncertainty again.

Pisceans are at home in any kind of creative or caring career. Many can be found in teaching, nursing and the arts. Some find life hard and are often unhappy; many have to make tremendous sacrifices on behalf of others. This may be a pattern which repeats itself from childhood, where the message is that the Piscean's needs always come last. These people can be stubborn, awkward, selfish and quite nasty when a friendship or relationship goes sour. This is because, despite their basically kind and gentle personality, there is a side which needs to be in charge of any relationship. Pisceans make extremely faithful partners as long as the romance doesn't evaporate and their partners treat them well. Problems occur if they are mistreated or rejected, if they become bored or restless or if their alcohol intake climbs over the danger level. The Piscean lover is a sexual fantasist, so in this sphere of life anything can happen!

You and Yours

What is it like to bring up an Arien child? What kind of father does a Libran make? How does it feel to grow up with a Sagittarian mother? Whatever your own sign is, how do you appear to your parents and how do you behave towards your children?

THE GEMINI FATHER

Gemini fathers are fairly laid back in their approach and, while they cope well with fatherhood, they can become bored with home life and try to escape from their duties. Some are so absorbed with work that they hardly see their offspring. At home, Gemini fathers will provide books, educational toys and as much computer equipment as the child can use, and they enjoy a family game of tennis.

THE GEMINI MOTHER

These mothers can be very pushy because they see education as the road to success. They encourage a child to pursue any interest and will sacrifice time and money for this. They usually have a job outside the home and may rely on other people to do some child-minding for them. Their children cannot always count on coming home to a balanced meal, but they can talk to their mothers on any subject.

THE GEMINI CHILD

These children needs a lot of reassurance because they often feel like square pegs in round holes. They either do very well at school and incur the wrath of less able children, or they fail dismally and have to make it up later in life. They learn to read early and some have excellent mechanical ability while others excel at sports. They get bored very easily and they can be extremely irritating.

THE ARIES FATHER

Arien men take the duties of fatherhood very seriously. They read to their children, take them on educational trips and expose them to art and music from an early age. They can push their children too hard or tyrannize the sensitive ones. The Aries father wants his children not only to have what he didn't have but also to be what he isn't. He respects those children who are high achievers and who can stand up to him.

THE ARIES MOTHER

Arien women love their children dearly and will make amazing sacrifices for them, but don't expect them to give up their jobs or their outside interests for motherhood. Competitive herself, this mother wants her children to be the best and she may push them too hard. However, she is kind-hearted, affectionate and not likely to over-discipline them. She treats her offspring as adults and is well loved in return.

THE ARIES CHILD

Arien children are hard to ignore. Lively, noisy and demanding, they try to enjoy every moment of their childhood. Despite this, they lack confidence and need reassurance. Often clever but lacking in self-discipline, they need to be made to attend school each day and to do their homework. Active and competitive, these children excel in sports, dancing or learning to play a pop music instrument.

THE TAURUS FATHER

This man cares deeply for his children and wants the best for them, but doesn't expect the impossible. He may lay the law down and he can be unsympathetic to the attitudes and interests of a new generation. He may frighten young children by shouting at them. Being a responsible parent, he offers a secure family base but he may find it hard to let them go when they want to leave.

THE TAURUS MOTHER

These women make good mothers due to their highly domesticated nature. Some are real earth mothers, baking bread and making wonderful toys and games for their children. Sane and sensible but not highly imaginative, they do best with a child who has ordinary needs and they get confused by those who are 'special' in any way. Taurus mothers are very loving but they use reasonable discipline when necessary.

THE TAURUS CHILD

Taurean children can be surprisingly demanding. Their loud voices and stubborn natures can be irritating. Plump, sturdy and strong, some are shy and retiring, while others can bully weaker children. Artistic, sensual and often musical, these children can lose themselves in creative or beautiful hobbies. They need to be encouraged to share and express love and also to avoid too many sweet foods.

THE CANCER FATHER

A true family man who will happily embrace even stepchildren as if they were his own. Letting go of the family when they grow up is another matter. Cancerian sulks, moodiness and bouts of childishness can confuse or frighten some children, while his changeable attitude to money can make them unsure of what they should ask for. This father enjoys domesticity and child-rearing and he may be happy to swap roles.

THE CANCER MOTHER

Cancerian women are excellent home makers and cheerful and reasonable mothers, as long as they have a part-time job or an interest outside the house. They instinctively know when a child is unhappy and can deal with it in a manner which is both efficient and loving. These women have a reputation for clinging but most are quite realistic when the time comes for their brood to leave the nest.

THE CANCER CHILD

These children are shy, cautious and slow to grow up. They may achieve little at school, 'disappearing' behind louder and more demanding classmates. They can be worriers who complain about every ache and pain or suffer from imaginary fears. They may take on the mother's role in the family, dictating to their sisters and brothers at times. Gentle and loving but moody and secretive, they need a lot of love and encouragement.

THE LEO FATHER

These men can be wonderful fathers as long as they remember that children are not simply small and rather obstreperous adults. Leo fathers like to be involved with their children and encourage them to do well at school. They happily make sacrifices for their children and they truly want them to have the best, but they can be a bit too strict and they may demand too high a standard.

THE LEO MOTHER

Leo mothers are very caring and responsible but they cannot be satisfied with a life of pure domesticity, and need to combine motherhood with a job. These mothers don't fuss about minor details. They're prepared to put up with a certain amount of noise and disruption, but they can be irritable and they may demand too much of their children.

THE LEO CHILD

These children know almost from the day they are born that they are special.

They are usually loved and wanted but they are also aware that a lot is expected from them. Leo children appear outgoing but they are surprisingly sensitive and easily hurt. They only seem to wake up to the need to study a day or so after they leave school, but they find a way to make a success of their lives.

THE VIRGO FATHER

These men may be embarrassed by open declarations of love and affection and find it hard to give cuddles and reassurance to small children. Yet they love their offspring dearly and will go to any lengths to see that they have the best possible education and outside activities. Virgoan men can become wrapped up in their work, forgetting to spend time relaxing and playing with their children.

THE VIRGO MOTHER

Virgoan women try hard to be good mothers because they probably had a poor childhood themselves. They love their children very much and want the best for them but they may be fussy about unnecessary details, such as dirt on the kitchen floor or the state of the children's school books. If they can keep their tensions and longings away from their children, they can be the most kindly and loving parents.

THE VIRGO CHILD

Virgoan children are practical and capable and can do very well at school, but they are not always happy. They don't always fit in and they may have difficulty making friends. They may be shy, modest and sensitive and they can find it hard to live up to their own impossibly high standards. Virgo children don't need harsh discipline, they want approval and will usually respond perfectly well to reasoned argument.

THE LIBRA FATHER

Libran men mean well, but they may not actually perform that well. They have no great desire to be fathers but welcome their children when they come along. They may slide out of the more irksome tasks by having an absorbing job or a series of equally absorbing hobbies which keep them occupied outside the home. These men do better with older children because they can talk to them.

THE LIBRA MOTHER

Libran mothers are pleasant and easy-going but some of them are more interested in their looks, their furnishings and their friends than their children. Others are very loving and kind but a bit too soft, which results in their children disrespecting them or walking all over them in later life. These mothers enjoy talking to their children and encouraging them to succeed.

THE LIBRA CHILD

These children are charming and attractive and they have no difficulty in getting on with people. They make just enough effort to get through school and only do the household jobs they cannot dodge. They may drive their parents mad with their demands for the latest gadget or gimmick. However, their common sense, sense of humour and reasonable attitude makes harsh discipline unnecessary.

THE SCORPIO FATHER

These fathers can be really awful or absolutely wonderful, and there aren't any half-measures. Good Scorpio men provide love and security because they stick closely to their homes and families and are unlikely to do a disappearing act. Difficult ones can be loud and tyrannical. These proud men want their children to be the best.

THE SCORPIO MOTHER

These mothers are either wonderful or not really maternal at all, although they try to do their best. If they take to child-rearing, they encourage their offspring educationally and in their hobbies. These mothers have no time for whiny or miserable children but they respect outgoing, talented and courageous ones, and can cope with a handful.

THE SCORPIO CHILD

Scorpio children are competitive, self-centred and unwilling to co-operate with brothers, sisters, teachers or anyone else when in an awkward mood. They can be deeply unreadable, living in a world of their own and filled with all kinds of strange angry feelings. At other times, they can be delightfully caring companions. They love animals, sports, children's organizations and group activities.

THE SAGITTARIUS FATHER

Sagittarian fathers will give their children all the education they can stand. They happily provide books, equipment and take their offspring out to see anything interesting. They may not always be available to their offspring, but they make up for it by surprising their families with tickets for sporting events or by bringing home a pet for the children. These men are cheerful and childlike themselves.

THE SAGITTARIUS MOTHER

This mother is kind, easy-going and pleasant. She may be very ordinary with suburban standards or she may be unbelievably eccentric, forcing the family to take up strange diets and filling the house with weird and wonderful people. Some opt out of child-rearing by finding childminders while others take on other people's children and a host of animals in addition to their own.

THE SAGITTARIUS CHILD

Sagittarian children love animals and the outdoor life but they are just as interested in sitting around and watching the telly as the next child. These children have plenty of friends whom they rush out and visit at every opportunity. Happy and optimistic but highly independent, they cannot be pushed in any direction. Many leave home in late their teens in order to travel.

THE CAPRICORN FATHER

These are true family men who cope with housework and child-rearing but they are sometimes too involved in work to spend much time at home. Dutiful and caring, these men are unlikely to run off with a bimbo or to leave their family wanting. However, they can be stuffy or out of touch with the younger generation. They encourage their children to do well and to behave properly.

THE CAPRICORN MOTHER

Capricorn women make good mothers but they may be inclined to fuss. Being ambitious, they want their children to do well and they teach them to respect teachers, youth leaders and so on. These mothers usually find work outside the home in order to supplement the family income. They are very loving but they can be too keen on discipline and the careful management of pocket money.

THE CAPRICORN CHILD

Capricorn children are little adults from the day they are born. They don't need much discipline or encouragement to do well at school. Modest and well behaved, they are almost too good to be true. However, they suffer badly with their nerves and can be prone to ailments such as asthma. They need to be taught to let go, have fun and enjoy their childhood. Some are too selfish or ambitious to make friends.

THE AQUARIAN FATHER

Some Aquarian men have no great desire to be fathers but they make a reasonable job of it when they have to. They cope best when their children are reasonable and intelligent but, if they are not, they tune out and ignore them. Some Aquarians will spend hours inventing games and toys for their children while all of them value education and try to push their children.

THE AQUARIAN MOTHER

Some of these mothers are too busy putting the world to rights to see what is going on in their own family. However, they are kind, reasonable and keen on education. They may be busy outside the house but they often take their children along with them. They are not fussy homemakers, and are happy to have all the neighbourhood kids in the house. They respect a child's dignity.

THE AQUARIAN CHILD

These children may be demanding when very young but they become much more reasonable when at school. They are easily bored and need outside interests. They have many friends and may spend more time in other people's homes than in their own. Very stubborn and determined, they make it quite clear from an early age that they intend to do things their own way. These children suffer from nerves.

THE PISCES FATHER

Piscean men fall into one of two categories. Some are kind and gentle, happy to take their children on outings and to introduce them to art, culture, music or sport. Others are disorganized and unpredictable. The kindly fathers don't always push their children. They encourage their kids to have friends and a pet or two.

THE PISCES MOTHER

Piscean mothers may be lax and absent-minded but they love their children and are usually loved in return. Many are too disorganized to run a perfect household so meals, laundry, etc. can be hit and miss, but their children prosper despite this, although many learn to reverse the mother/child roles. These mothers teach their offspring to appreciate animals and the environment.

THE PISCES CHILD

These sensitive children may find life difficult and they can get lost among stronger, more demanding brothers and sisters. They may drive their parents batty with their dreamy attitude and they can make a fuss over nothing. They need a secure and loving home with parents who shield them from harsh reality while encouraging them to develop their imaginative and psychic abilities.

Your Rising Sign

WHAT IS A RISING SIGN?

Your rising sign is the sign of the zodiac which was climbing up over the eastern horizon the moment you were born. This is not the same as your Sun sign; your Sun sign depends upon your date of birth, but your rising sign depends upon the time of day that you were born, combined with your date and place of birth.

The rising sign modifies your Sun sign character quite considerably, so when you have worked out which is your rising sign, read pages 39–40 to see how it modifies your Sun sign. Then take a deeper look by going back to 'All the Other Sun Signs' on page 21 and read the relevant Sun sign material there to discover more about your ascendant (rising sign) nature.

One final point is that the sign that is opposite your rising sign (or 'ascendant') is known as your 'descendant'. This shows what you want from other people, and it may give a clue as to your choice of friends, colleagues and lovers (see pages 41–3). So once you have found your rising sign and read the character interpretation, check out the character reading for your descendant to see what you are looking for in others.

How to Begin

Read through this section while following the example below. Even if you only have a vague idea of your birth time, you won't find this method difficult; just go for a rough time of birth and then read the Sun sign information for that sign to see if it fits your personality. If you seem to be more like the sign that comes before or after it, then it is likely that you were born a little earlier or later than your assumed time of birth. Don't forget to deduct an hour for summertime births.

1. Look at the illustration top right. You will notice that it has the time of day arranged around the outer circle. It looks a bit like a clock face, but it is different because it shows the whole 24-hour day in two-hour blocks.

2. Write the astrological symbol that represents the Sun (a circle with a dot in the middle) in the segment that corresponds to your time of birth. (If you were born during Daylight Saving or British Summer Time, deduct one hour from your birth time.) Our example shows someone who was born between 2 a.m. and 4 a.m.

3. Now write the name of your sign or the symbol for your sign on the line which is at the end of the block of time that your Sun falls into. Our example shows a person who was born between 2 a.m. and 4 a.m. under the sign of Pisces.

4. Either write in the names of the zodiac signs or use the symbols in their correct order (see the key below) around the chart in an anti-clockwise direction, starting from the line which is at the start of the block of time that your sun falls into.

5. The sign that appears on the left-hand side of the wheel at the 'Dawn' line is your rising sign, or ascendant. The example shows a person born with the Sun in Pisces and with Aquarius rising. Incidentally, the example chart also shows Leo, which falls on the 'Dusk' line, in the descendant. You will always find the ascendant sign on the 'Dawn' line and the descendant sign on the 'Dusk' line.

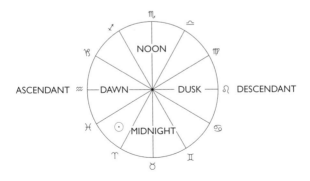

♈ Aries	♋ Cancer	♎ Libra	♑ Capricorn
♉ Taurus	♌ Leo	♏ Scorpio	♒ Aquarius
♊ Gemini	♍ Virgo	♐ Sagittarius	♓ Pisces

Here is another example for you to run through, just to make sure that you have grasped the idea correctly. This example is for a more awkward time of birth, being exactly on the line between two different blocks of time. This example is for a person with a Capricorn Sun sign who was born at 10 a.m.

1. The Sun is placed exactly on the 10 a.m. line.

2. The sign of Capricorn is placed on the 10 a.m. line.

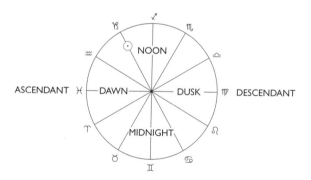

3. All the other signs are placed in astrological order (anti-clockwise) around the chart.

4. This person has the Sun in Capricorn and Pisces rising, and therefore with Virgo on the descendant.

Using the Rising Sign Finder

Please bear in mind that this method is approximate. If you want to be really sure of your rising sign, you should contact an astrologer. However, this system will work with reasonable accuracy wherever you were born. Check out the Sun and ascendant combination in the following pages. Once you've done so, if you're not quite sure you've got it right, you should also read the Sun sign character readings on pages 21–8 for the signs both before and after the rising sign you think is yours. Rising signs are such an obvious part of one's personality that one quick glance will show you which one belongs to you.

Can Your Rising Sign Tell You More about Your Future?

When it comes to tracking events, the rising sign is equal in importance to the Sun sign. So, if you want a more accurate forecast when reading newspapers or magazines, you should read the horoscope for your rising sign as well as your Sun sign. In the case of books such as this, you should really treat yourself to two: one to correspond with your rising sign, and another for your usual Sun sign, and read both each day!

How Your Rising Sign Modifies Your Sun Sign

GEMINI WITH ARIES RISING You could have a very outgoing personality with the ability to inspire others but you may not be too tactful.

GEMINI WITH TAURUS RISING You could have a real head for figures, choosing to work as an accountant or a banker. You are keen on art, music and craftwork.

GEMINI WITH GEMINI RISING Your childhood difficulties take a long time to shake off and you may have to wait until middle age to reach your potential. If you are born before dawn, you will have more confidence than if you are born after dawn.

GEMINI WITH CANCER RISING You are quieter and more gentle than the average Gemini and you are probably drawn to one of the caring professions but you like money too.

GEMINI WITH LEO RISING You need a good standard of living and you probably work hard to create this. You get on well with all kinds of people and you are particularly fond of young people.

GEMINI WITH VIRGO RISING You are an excellent communicator with a talent for language, teaching or writing. You can drive yourself crazy worrying about nothing.

GEMINI WITH LIBRA RISING You are great company and you are always bang up-to-date in your thinking. You could make a success of a career in the legal profession or as an international business person.

GEMINI WITH SCORPIO RISING You are far more intense than the average Gemini and you can feel passionate about your beliefs. Your childhood could have left you with a fear of abandonment or of financial insecurity.

GEMINI WITH SAGITTARIUS RISING You seek to protect your personal freedom and you may find it hard to settle down into a conventional lifestyle. You are very excited by ideas and travel.

GEMINI WITH CAPRICORN RISING You are one of the world's hardest workers, being ambitious for yourself and your family. You may have suffered poverty or deprivation in childhood.

GEMINI WITH AQUARIUS RISING You are excited by ideas and you may choose a lifestyle which allows you to explore them. You make a career in some form of communications.

GEMINI WITH PISCES RISING You are quieter and more home-loving than the average Gemini and you could also be drawn to mystical or psychic matters. You may choose to work from home.

Gemini in Love

YOU NEED:

RELIABILITY You have had enough unreliable people in your life to appreciate a sane and stable partner. Your lover should be calm and unflappable and able to cope with your nerves and depression.

SAFETY Gemini women can attract violent partners, so you must make sure that you see the signs of this on the way before you get trapped. Gemini men need a woman who is a little motherly and who gives them a sense of security.

VARIETY You are easily bored, so a partner who has a very regular routine to his life and no imagination wouldn't suit you at all. You need someone who will spring little surprises on you and take you out regularly.

YOU GIVE:

REASSURANCE You know what it is to feel insecure and unprotected, so you do your best to make a partner feel that life is under control and that you can cope. You may be moody but you are always there.

VARIETY You won't bore your partner by always being the same; you like to vary everything from meals to lifestyle to lovemaking. You are always ready for an outing or to meet interesting people.

ENCOURAGEMENT You stand by and encourage a lover in all their schemes and you stand by them even when things don't work out entirely as expected.

WHAT YOU CAN EXPECT FROM THE OTHER ZODIAC SIGNS:

ARIES *Truth, honesty, playfulness.* You can expect an open and honest relationship with no hidden agendas. Your Arien lover will be a bit childish at times, however.

TAURUS *Security, stability, comfort.* Taureans will stand by you and try to improve your financial position. They will create beautiful homes and gardens for their partners.

CANCER *Emotional security, companionship, help.* Cancerians will never leave you stranded at a party or alone when suffering form the flu. They always lend a hand when asked.

LEO *Affection, fun, loyalty.* Leo lovers are very steadfast and they would avenge anyone who hurt one of their family. They enjoy romping and playing affectionate love games.

VIRGO *Clear-thinking, kindness, humour.* Virgoans make intelligent and amusing partners. They can be critical but are never unkind. They take their responsibility towards you seriously.

LIBRA *Fair-play, sensuality, advice.* Librans will listen to your problems and give balanced and sensible advice. They are wonderfully inventive and are affectionate lovers too.

SCORPIO *Truth, passion, loyalty.* Scorpios will take your interests as seriously as they do their own. They will stick by you when the going gets tough and they wont flannel you.

SAGITTARIUS *Honesty, fun, novelty.* Theses lovers will never bore you and they'll keep up with whatever pace you set. They seek the truth and they donít keep their feelings hidden.

CAPRICORN *Companionship, common sense, laughter.* Capricorns enjoy doing things together and they won't leave you in the lurch when the going gets tough. They can make you laugh too.

AQUARIUS *Stimulation, friendship, sexuality.* Aquarians are friends as well as lovers. They are great fun because you never know what they are going to do next, in or out of bed.

PISCES *Sympathy, support, love.* These romantic lovers never let you down. They can take you with them into their personal fantasy world and they are always ready for a laugh.

WHICH SIGN ARE YOU COMPATIBLE WITH?

GEMINI/ARIES
Good combination unless the Arien is too bossy or selfish.

GEMINI/TAURUS
You either complement each other well or can't stand each other.

GEMINI/GEMINI
Either mutual understanding or both demanding attention at once.

GEMINI/CANCER
Cancer will mother Gemini and Gemini will love it.

GEMINI/LEO
Gemini provides inspiration for Leo, Leo protects Gemini.

GEMINI/VIRGO
Many shared interests but both may lack common sense.

GEMINI/LIBRA
Either excellent combination or both looking for too much.

GEMINI/SCORPIO
Scorpio will dominate Gemini, both will use sarcasm to score points.

GEMINI/SAGITTARIUS
Sagittarius makes Gemini laugh and
they share mental interests.

GEMINI/AQUARIUS
Excellent combination as long as
Aquarius is not too detached.

GEMINI/CAPRICORN
Not a bad combination, especially
for business.

GEMINI/PISCES
Pisces can irritate Gemini but this
can work nevertheless.

Your Prospects for 1999

LOVE

With Chiron, Pluto opposing your Sun sign this year and with Mars joining
them from the 3rd of September to the 18th of October, nothing regarding
your relationship situation will be straightforward. Many of you will now be
in a settled relationship which gives real meaning to your life but you could
also be hedged about by outside problems that make the relationship hard to
handle. For example, there may be financial or health setbacks that have to
be lived through and the words 'for richer and for poorer, in sickness and in
health' will come back to remind you of your commitment. However, all is
far from being gloom and doom; it is just that other people or other
circumstances may dictate what happens within your closest relationships
this year. In the past, you may have suffered financial losses or even swindles
as a result of trusting the wrong people. However, now you will find business,
financial and other kinds of partnerships less confusing. Single Geminis have
the chance of an on-and-off affair early in the year and it is possible that your
lover could leave you thinking that it is all over, only to drift back again during
the last three months of 1999. If one brief affair ends by mid-year, another
could start after the end of August.

MONEY AND WORK

It looks as though work and money may be two completely separate issues
for you this year because although there is evidence of your working life
being much more successful than before, this may not actually bring financial
increases. Money and other forms of luck could come through a variety of
unusual sources. Friends will put in a good a word or two for you while an
involvement in a club, society or group activity will also bring some
unexpected benefits. May and June look like being good months for money

matters but you will have to guard against unexpected expenses later in the year. Look for unexpected or unusual sources of income this year and don't rule out the possibility of doing two part-time jobs or a variety of odd and unusual things to bring in the pennies. The very start and the very end of the year could bring unexpected gifts or windfalls. Workwise, there will be plenty of ups and downs and you may have to deal with a difficult man in connection with work at times during the first half of the year. The end of the year will be a time of rewards and financial benefits from work but this too will be hedged about by muddle and delays. You may be attracted to a spare-time job in the fields of health and healing.

HEALTH

This year Mars will spend a longer than usual amount of time in the sign of Scorpio and as this represents the health area of your chart, this will have an effect on you. On the one hand, Mars endows energy and enterprise so you will feel more vigorous and more alive than is usual but, on the other hand, Mars can lead to fevers and also accidents due to rashness or momentary losses of concentration. The worst times will be from March to early May while the best times will be from up to the 3rd of March and then again from early July until early September. Chesty ailments will need to be watched towards the end of the year, especially during November.

FAMILY AND HOME

Family and domestic matters will cause you less aggravation this year than is usually the case. There may be worries in connection with a father figure during March but that will soon blow over. A very minor setback will occur in your household during the first couple of weeks of August but this too soon passes. On the whole, both household and family matters should be easy and trouble-free this year and there is no evidence of house moves or other major upheavals of a domestic nature. If you have people to stay or if you entertain at home, this will all be rather jolly so enjoy your home life to the full in 1999

LUCK

Luck will come through friends, group activities and through anything of an educational nature. If you decide to study or to train for something new, this will be a success. Out-of-the-blue windfalls and strokes of luck are possible this year and it seems that at least some of your dreams will come true. You will have the knack of being in the right place at the right time when it really matters.

The Aspects and their Astrological Meanings

CONJUNCT   This shows important events which are usually, but not always, good.

SEXTILE   Good, particularly for work and mental activity.

SQUARE   Difficult, challenging.

TRINE   Great for romance, family life and creativity.

OPPOSITE   Awkward, depressing, challenging.

INTO   This shows when a particular planet enters a new sign of the zodiac, thus setting off a new phase or a new set of circumstances.

DIRECT   When a planet resumes normal direct motion.

RETROGRADE   When a planet apparently begins to go backwards.

VOID   When the Moon makes no aspect to any planet.

September at a Glance

LOVE	♥			
WORK	★			
MONEY	£	£		
HEALTH	✪	✪	✪	✪
LUCK	♘			

TUESDAY, 1ST SEPTEMBER
Moon trine Saturn

You'll do best if you are self-reliant today. You could spot a detail that will enable you to make some money, but you'll only do this if you are left to your own devices.

WEDNESDAY, 2ND SEPTEMBER
Void Moon

The term 'void of course' means that neither the Moon nor any of the other planets is making any important aspects during the course of its travels today. When this kind of day occurs, the worst thing you can do is launch a new venture. Stick to routine tasks wherever possible.

THURSDAY, 3RD SEPTEMBER
Moon conjunct Neptune

Neither a borrower or a lender be – that's your motto today under the influence of the Moon and Neptune. Don't allow yourself to be persuaded to part with cash on any pretext whatsoever. If in doubt plead poverty or, better still, make yourself scarce!

FRIDAY, 4TH SEPTEMBER
Mars opposite Uranus

A serious crisis of faith is due today as Mars and Uranus engage in a mental tussle, with your conscience as the prize. You may feel confused as old convictions fade away and new, but more disturbing, ideas come to mind. You need to think in a calm and controlled manner, but this may be difficult while you are so excitable. On the same theme, take extra care when travelling.

GEMINI

SATURDAY, 5TH SEPTEMBER
Moon opposite Venus

You and your beloved could find yourselves out of harmony about something. Perhaps you can't agree about holiday plans or travel in general could be the cause of the upset. For example, one of you may feel that you should visit the family or take a business trip just when the other one wants you to be home.

SUNDAY, 6TH SEPTEMBER
Full Moon eclipse

The Lunar eclipse today could bring a great deal of tension into your life. The problem may be related to parental figures or older members of the family, but it could just as easily be a culmination of work and home problems. You cannot ignore this situation. Something will have to be done, and you'll need to find a way to do it soon.

MONDAY, 7TH SEPTEMBER
Moon sextile Neptune

Your sensitive handling of a delicate situation will find favour with bosses and other authority figures today. This could be an opportunity for career advancement or a raise of some kind.

TUESDAY, 8TH SEPTEMBER
Mercury into Virgo

Your life will be extremely busy for a while now, with little time to sit around and rest. You will have more to do with friends, relatives, colleagues and neighbours than usual and you could spend time sorting out minor domestic and work problems with various tradespeople. A vehicle may also need your attention.

WEDNESDAY, 9TH SEPTEMBER
Mercury trine Saturn

A private chat with someone you respect such as a parent or other older relative will help alleviate certain anxieties that have plagued you. This conversation will soon put everything into perspective and you'll know exactly what to do next.

THURSDAY, 10TH SEPTEMBER
Venus trine Saturn

Wednesday's influence continues today as a sense of parental guidance is evident, for which you'll be thankful. Sober common sense will help you understand your own family situation.

FRIDAY, 11TH SEPTEMBER
Mercury conjunct Venus

A comfortable atmosphere pervades your home today. Mercury is closely linked with Venus in the domestic area of your chart, so this is a good time to show hospitality and enjoy good company on your own territory. Family and friends will be a source of comfort.

SATURDAY, 12TH SEPTEMBER
Moon sextile Mars

This is a good day to go shopping for any form of transport. This may be a matter of renting a set of skis for your winter holiday or actually buying a new car. The same goes for any kind of tools, especially if they move along in some way, like a jigsaw or even a chisel. If you have to travel by public transport, you may find a better route for your usual journeys.

SUNDAY, 13TH SEPTEMBER
Moon square Jupiter

Be realistic! That's the astral message today as the strong influence of Jupiter encourages you to take an overly optimistic view of nearly everything. You could take on far more than you can comfortably handle in a work situation.

MONDAY, 14TH SEPTEMBER
Moon sextile Venus

There's no doubt that you're a person of impeccable taste. Your sense of style as you furnish your surroundings and rearrange the furniture to better effect will be awe-inspiring! You're determined to make your home as comfortable and luxurious as possible. Expect visitors to drop in, if only to admire your handiwork.

TUESDAY, 15TH SEPTEMBER
Moon sextile Sun

This is an excellent day to buy goodies for the home. So if your curtains need replacing or if the dog has chewed the cushion covers just one time too many, take yourself out to the shops and see what you can do about it.

WEDNESDAY, 16TH SEPTEMBER
Sun opposite Jupiter

On the surface this seems to be an excellent time to press ahead with your most cherished ambitions. But hold on – are you sure that you're not taking too much on trust alone? Do you think that your luck is going to hold forever? Perhaps you're relying on a relative to help you out, yet shouldn't you talk it over with them first? Don't make too many assumptions now. Check your facts again.

THURSDAY, 17TH SEPTEMBER
Moon conjunct Mars

There may be some quite interesting news about relatives or neighbours today. This is a good day for communications of all kinds, whether with family members or anyone outside your immediate circle. If you need to contact tradespeople, now is an auspicious time to do it.

FRIDAY, 18TH SEPTEMBER
Moon trine Saturn

Visits from your parents or other relatives will bring you joy and happiness now. All your family relationships should be calm and pleasant.

SATURDAY, 19TH SEPTEMBER
Mercury opposite Jupiter

It's going to be a rocky day on which garbled messages, misunderstandings and over-reactions abound. Be as calm as possible and don't let work or family stress get you down.

SUNDAY, 20TH SEPTEMBER
New Moon

The New Moon in the area of domestic life and heritage shows that memories of childhood become very important now. Things learned then may now be questioned as you look back and try to relate happenings in early life to events today. You must admit that the world has changed immeasurably, so some concepts are rather dated. On the other hand, firm values passed down to you are as valid now as they ever were. Of course, you have to work out the difference for yourself.

MONDAY, 21ST SEPTEMBER
Moon sextile Pluto

This should be a pleasant day with a chance for at least one loving cuddle with that special person. Fortunately your partner's mood is just as amorous as your own, so enjoy all this love and affection while the going is good.

TUESDAY, 22ND SEPTEMBER
Sun trine Neptune

It's quite a nostalgic time for you as the Sun makes contact with impressionable

Neptune. You'll be happiest within your own surroundings, reviewing happy memories. This sounds like a good day to get out the photo albums and reminisce.

WEDNESDAY, 23RD SEPTEMBER
Sun into Libra

The Sun's movement into your fifth Solar house shows that you've had enough of being dutiful and working your fingers to the bone. You now desperately need some fun, so it won't do you any harm to please yourself for the next month or so. Think of something you really enjoy and go for it. Artistic ventures of all kinds, whether dramatic, poetic, literary or just the a love of a good film, should be pursued. Indulge yourself to the full – you'll feel all the better for it.

THURSDAY, 24TH SEPTEMBER
Mercury into Libra

Over the next two or three weeks something will capture your attention and keep you amused. You may take an interest in intellectual games such as bridge, chess or other board games. You may stimulate the grey cells by doing quizzes or crosswords, and there's also a fair chance you could win a competition. Read ahead to find the best days for lucky chances.

FRIDAY, 25TH SEPTEMBER
Sun conjunct Mercury

If ever there was a day for an amorous heart-to-heart, this is it! The Sun unites with Mercury, making intimate conversation and declarations of love so much easier. Don't waste this tender opportunity to express your love. You'll be a witty and amusing companion this Friday.

SATURDAY, 26TH SEPTEMBER
Moon conjunct Pluto

One particular relationship is undergoing important changes, and things may never be quite the same again. It looks as if this is a change for the better, even if you do decide to break up with someone. You may transform the way you deal with others and try to make difficult partnerships workable.

SUNDAY, 27TH SEPTEMBER
Mercury sextile Pluto

If you thought you were the shy type, you could surprise yourself today. The passion you convey in a few breathless words will be staggering. Ardent affections are about to be exchanged. Who knows what steamy excitement may follow?

MONDAY, 28TH SEPTEMBER
Moon trine Saturn

You won't be in the most sociable of moods today. Perhaps there's some serious financial matter that needs your undivided attention. You won't be happy until it's out of the way, so seclude yourself and get on with it.

TUESDAY, 29TH SEPTEMBER
Sun sextile Pluto

The aspect between the Sun and Pluto could transform your personal life. Those who are married or otherwise linked will find that relationships enter a new phase. Single Geminis could find the love of their lives!

WEDNESDAY, 30TH SEPTEMBER
Venus into Libra

The two themes that are likely to be important in the short-term future are those of children and having a good time. We hope that these two are compatible.

October at a Glance

LOVE	❤	❤	❤	❤	❤
WORK	★	★	★		
MONEY	£	£	£	£	£
HEALTH	✚	✚	✚		
LUCK	♘	♘	♘	♘	♘

THURSDAY, 1ST OCTOBER
Sun trine Uranus

Your emotions will be stirred today as you suddenly fall head over heels in love with an unusually attractive person. This experience should be electric yet short-lived. Indeed, this infatuation may have gone off the boil by the end of the day and, instead of being whisked off to someone's boudoir, you could finish up in bed with a good book and a cup of cocoa!

GEMINI

FRIDAY, 2ND OCTOBER
Moon opposite Mars

You may think you are talking perfect sense but everyone else will be on a completely different wavelength. This may be due to the battle of the sexes or, let us say, the difference in thinking that is inherent in males and females. In short, you may not be able to get your man or woman to see things your way.

SATURDAY, 3RD OCTOBER
Moon square Pluto

It is no good trying to throw your weight around today because it won't be appreciated by your superiors at work or by your loved ones at home. One of the reasons for your frustration is that it will be hard for you to reach even the most modest goals today. An older woman may irritate you or, worse still, you could temporarily sink into a strangely negative frame of mind.

SUNDAY, 4TH OCTOBER
Moon conjunct Jupiter

There's a marvellous, uplifting atmosphere every time the Moon meets up with Jupiter. Now you'll be prepared to cast the cares of the world behind you and indulge in some well-deserved pleasure. You'll have all the more reason to celebrate when an employer or even a prospective boss takes you aside to heap praise upon you. People you meet today should do your worldly prospects some good.

MONDAY, 5TH OCTOBER
Venus sextile Pluto

We hope that your energy levels are high because the passionate intensity revealed by today's stars show that physical action is a probability. The combination of loving Venus and intense Pluto spells a session of steamy sensuality.

TUESDAY, 6TH OCTOBER
Full Moon

The Full Moon could make you feel a bit tetchy and tense and also bring you expense that, when you come to think of it, is only to be expected. Keep your own counsel and look on the bright side.

WEDNESDAY, 7TH OCTOBER
Mars into Virgo

Mars enters your Solar fourth house today, focusing your attention on the home and family for a few weeks. You may have a lot to do in the house and it's possible that you will be surrounded by tradespeople for a while. You may also decide to replace outworn items of equipment. Mars is associated with sharp objects and engineering, so you may do some work on a vehicle.

THURSDAY, 8TH OCTOBER
Moon sextile Jupiter

There's some unexpected good fortune in the stars today. The powerful influence of Jupiter opens up new doorways in your career, while a decision made behind closed doors should enhance your chances of professional success. There is certainly a person in a position of authority who is well disposed towards you.

FRIDAY, 9TH OCTOBER
Moon trine Uranus

You'll be in an excellent mood today. Your personality shines and your originality is obvious for all to see. You may feel rather restless and dissatisfied with the normal run of things, but this is only to be expected from such a supreme individualist.

SATURDAY, 10TH OCTOBER
Mars trine Saturn

If you need any help or advice over a practical matter in the home, a man will have the answers. Women won't be able to help you at the moment, so hunt down the opposite sex!

SUNDAY, 11TH OCTOBER
Neptune direct

Neptune turns to direct motion today, making it easier to cope with all kinds of relationships. You may have been so blinded by love that you've been crediting your lover with characteristics that he or she doesn't have. On the other hand, you may have been blaming someone falsely or laying all the ills of the world at someone else's doorstep. Today's influence should help you see the truth of the matter.

MONDAY, 12TH OCTOBER
Mercury into Scorpio

Mercury moves into the area of your chart that deals with duties and health. This suggests that if you have been feeling ill you will soon recover. Mercury is associated with healing, so the chances are that any health problems affecting you and your loved ones will soon pass.

TUESDAY, 13TH OCTOBER
Moon square Mercury

This will be a changeable day, so double-check everything that is said to you. Check on bank and money matters and try to keep a grip on important messages and bits of paper. If you are likely to travel around a bit today, stay tuned to your local radio station for traffic updates. If you have to negotiate with anyone, do so in person or by phone rather than by letter.

WEDNESDAY, 14TH OCTOBER
Mercury sextile Mars

It's a housework day, but before you despair we'll just add that you will not be alone in this long and thankless task. In fact, you'll whip your family into shape and apportion the jobs in order of difficulty. You may be a domestic tyrant, but you'll get things done!

THURSDAY, 15TH OCTOBER
Moon trine Saturn

If ever there was a day to stick close to your home patch, this is it! With the Moon and Saturn emphasizing privacy and comfort, you'll be doing yourself no favours if you stray too far. If you can possibly contain your impulsive nature, put your feet up and relax. If not, potter around and catch up on all those neglected household chores.

FRIDAY, 16TH OCTOBER
Moon square Pluto

With the best will in the world you won't be able to please everyone today. Your partner and family will all want their own way, and will go to extreme lengths to get it! If you want peace, leave the home and let everyone get on with their arguments without you.

SATURDAY, 17TH OCTOBER
Mercury square Uranus

Your restlessness and boredom could have far-reaching consequences today. If your job is too tedious, you're likely just to walk out and do something far more interesting. If that's the case, we just hope you can pacify your boss on your return!

SUNDAY, 18TH OCTOBER
Uranus direct

Uranus moves into direct motion today, ending a period of uncertainty and unpleasant surprises. In your case this seems to have been associated with overseas matters, so if your far-away friends or relatives have been experiencing difficulties, things should soon improve for them. Any problems associated with religion or the law will also be resolved.

MONDAY, 19TH OCTOBER
Mars square Pluto

Try to avoid confrontations with other family members today. Your partner and your parents may not see eye to eye, or perhaps your partner may find his or her own parents difficult to deal with. Try to keep calm and steer clear of jealous rows or manipulative behaviour.

TUESDAY, 20TH OCTOBER
New Moon

This month's New Moon is in an area of your chart that deals with creativity, so if there is something you want to do in the artistic field this is the time to get started. For some of you this could be as important as making a home, starting a family or launching a business enterprise. Younger members of the family could also show signs of talent.

WEDNESDAY, 21ST OCTOBER
Moon square Uranus

You may have envisaged a quiet, relaxing day, but the stars think otherwise. The Moon aspects Uranus, ensuring that anything can happen – and probably will! A sudden urge to treat yourself to a night out could stretch your bank balance to the limit. You know that splashing out isn't really wise, but you won't really care. Although you may be content to live for the day, try to moderate the spending just a little. A sudden romantic attraction is also shown for some.

THURSDAY, 22ND OCTOBER
Sun square Neptune

If you've been feeling somewhat downhearted, try so do something to cheer yourself up. Escape from the chores for a walk in the park, take your partner to see a show or a movie, or join a group of friends at your local club. It will do you the world of good.

FRIDAY, 23RD OCTOBER
Sun into Scorpio

The movement of the Sun into your Solar sixth house of work signals a period of success in your endeavours. Whatever you do will have a patina of success and glamour about it, and you will be the envy of other less fortunate or hard-working souls. Don't allow their envy to diminish your confidence.

SATURDAY, 24TH OCTOBER
Venus into Scorpio

Any squabbles at work should be resolved by the entry of Venus into your Solar house of habits, effort and service to others. Colleagues will get on better with each other from now on, for a spirit of harmony is as important in the workplace as in your home. If you're self-employed or earn your living by means of your wits, the presence of Venus is very encouraging for your future prospects. You'll find that the influence of women takes on added importance from now on.

SUNDAY, 25TH OCTOBER
Saturn into Pisces retrograde

The return of ringed Saturn to your area of ambitions puts many of your aims on hold, halting your progress. You may find it difficult to adapt to new circumstances because you're too fond of old, traditional ways.

MONDAY, 26TH OCTOBER
Sun conjunct Venus

The Sun makes a highly fortunate conjunction with Venus today, ushering in a time of prosperity and opportunity in your career. Those involved in the arts, music, cosmetic or beauty industries will benefit most, but the money-minded won't do so badly, either. Use your personal flair to ease your forward path! A professional woman will appreciate your talents and aid your ambitions.

TUESDAY, 27TH OCTOBER
Moon sextile Mercury

You and your partner should concentrate on the fun side of life today because neither of you will have your minds set on serious matters. If you spend the day alone you will find it hard to get down to anything important, so give yourself time off to read a novel, have a soak in the tub or otherwise indulge yourself. You won't want to tackle anything mentally daunting today.

WEDNESDAY, 28TH OCTOBER
Moon square Sun

The boring drudgery of day-to-day life won't be your cup of tea today, and you'd give almost anything to fly off to a more exotic location. Even if you can't manage that, you can always dream!

THURSDAY, 29TH OCTOBER
Saturn square Neptune

Career pressures affecting you or your partner may be particularly intense at the moment. This could cause a strain on your relationship, so it's vital that both of you give each other understanding and support to ease the burden.

FRIDAY, 30TH OCTOBER
Moon sextile Saturn

This is a good time to get down to a long-term project. Make a start now and you'll eventually see it through to the end and reap the rewards of your efforts. If you are on the brink of making a commitment to a relationship, then this seems destined to last. The same goes for a work- or business-related matter.

SATURDAY, 31ST OCTOBER
Moon conjunct Jupiter

It's a day for socializing, and this should also benefit your career. A party in the company of those you work for or respect will improve your prospects, as they'll be impressed by your dazzling generosity and bonhomie.

November at a Glance

LOVE	❤	❤	❤	
WORK	★			
MONEY	£	£	£	
HEALTH	✚			
LUCK	♘	♘		

SUNDAY, 1ST NOVEMBER
Mercury into Sagittarius

Mercury moves into your Solar seventh house of relationships today, emphasizing your dealings with others. This is a good time to get together with others for practical purposes, and it's also a wonderful time to start a relationship with that special someone. If you need to put the romance back into your marriage or communicate your feelings to a lover, do so now.

MONDAY, 2ND NOVEMBER
Void Moon

There are no important planetary aspects today and even the Moon is unaspected. This kind of a day is called a 'void of course Moon' day, because the Moon is void of aspects during this part of its course. The best way to approach such a day is to do what is normal and natural and rest if you can.

TUESDAY, 3RD NOVEMBER
Moon square Neptune

Don't be too ready to lend cash or pick up the tab today. You could be easily taken advantage of by an unscrupulous acquaintance, so take care and put your own needs first.

WEDNESDAY, 4TH NOVEMBER
Full Moon

Apart from a Full Moon today there is not much going on in the planetary scene. Therefore, rest and relax, take it easy and do only what you really have to do. You may feel the need to examine your heart and mind, embarking on an inner journey to analyse your actions and options as things stand. This may result in a few changes being made.

THURSDAY, 5TH NOVEMBER
Moon trine Neptune

Unseen forces seem to be working in your favour and you could find yourself getting on much better in life. You may, for example, have friends in high places who are beavering away on your behalf. You could just as easily attract the attention of a new and exciting lover, simply by being in the right place at the right time. The message here is that you won't have to work hard at anything to make it work today.

FRIDAY, 6TH NOVEMBER
Mercury conjunct Pluto

Keeping the lines of communication open between you and your partner is of vital importance today. Choose your words carefully and you'll resolve deep matters and troubling issues from the past. By the end of the day you'll wonder what the disagreement was about in the first place!

SATURDAY, 7TH NOVEMBER
Mars opposite Jupiter

It is too easy for minor hassles to be blown out of proportion today. The Martial opposition to Jupiter encourages you to jump to conclusions, lose your temper and snap at those who are closest to you both at home and at work. Try to keep cool.

SUNDAY, 8TH NOVEMBER
Venus trine Jupiter

By the end of today you should be smiling, since Venus and Jupiter bode well for all professional aims. There won't be a better time to try for promotion or seek a more fulfilling job. If you happen to be self-employed, a new contract should promote financial profit. Your natural charm will turn opportunities to your advantage.

MONDAY, 9TH NOVEMBER
Venus sextile Mars

A sense of harmony and contentment prevails today both at home and in the workplace. The excellent aspect between Venus and Mars ensures success in whatever you do, especially if taste and personal flair is involved. If you're lucky, romance may bloom among the filing cabinets!

TUESDAY, 10TH NOVEMBER
Sun trine Jupiter

Good news is on the way. Maybe there will be a little more money coming in, in the form of a bonus or a raise in pay. Another possibility is that you will soon have a chance to take a longed-for journey.

WEDNESDAY, 11TH NOVEMBER
Moon square Venus

Your imagination will be flying high but you will have difficulty translating your wonderful ideas into concrete results. You'll find it easier to get on with colleagues, associates and acquaintances than with your nearest and dearest today, and you may find yourself being admired by outsiders while your family considers you a dunce.

THURSDAY, 12TH NOVEMBER
Moon square Pluto

With the Moon in square aspect to Pluto it's likely that you'll drop something important on the floor, so make sure you have a soapy cloth near by to mop up the spills! When out of the kitchen you may hear news that is private or even secret. There will be good reason to respect the wishes of the messenger, so keep the information to yourself.

GEMINI

FRIDAY, 13TH NOVEMBER
Jupiter direct

The professional scene has been slow-going ever since Jupiter started to go backwards. However, from today the giant planet resumes a direct course to boost all your ambitions. There will be many opportunities to improve your worldly position, so prepare to make the most of every one of them.

SATURDAY, 14TH NOVEMBER
Sun sextile Mars

You will have plenty to do in the home today, but somehow you'll manage to enjoy this. For example, you may triumph over a pile of ironing while watching a lovely old 'weepy' on the television.

SUNDAY, 15TH NOVEMBER
Moon sextile Mercury

This is a great day to enjoy the company of friends and family alike, and if you can fit in some kind of entertainment or celebration so much the better. Tell your lover just how much he or she means to you and enjoy the closeness that today's aspect brings. If you are lonely and don't have a lover, get out and about because your chances of meeting someone worthwhile are very good at this time.

MONDAY, 16TH NOVEMBER
Moon opposite Saturn

You may find yourself out of sorts with other generations of the family. It may be your parents or your in-laws who get you down today or perhaps children are being impossible. There could be very little opportunity for escape, and freedom will seem far away. Try to find some time for yourself.

TUESDAY, 17TH NOVEMBER
Venus into Sagittarius

You are beginning to take a less personal and intense view of your closest partnerships, beginning to see your lover in honest terms rather than endowing them with attributes they simply don't have. This doesn't mean that you love them any less, it's just that you can be less exacting and begin to enjoy your relationship even more.

WEDNESDAY, 18TH NOVEMBER
Moon trine Jupiter

If you've been unwell or overburdened by work, the Lunar aspect to Jupiter brings welcome relief today. Health improves and your vigour will be restored.

GEMINI

THURSDAY, 19TH NOVEMBER
New Moon

This is definitely a time for very positive new beginnings in connection with work. You could look for a new job now or even receive promotion or a raise in salary. You seem to be more interested in work-related matters now than for some time past, and your imagination may be captured by some kind of money-making scheme. You could also find a way to make your working life easier.

FRIDAY, 20TH NOVEMBER
Mercury square Jupiter

You should get a clue that someone very close isn't pursuing the wisest course at the moment. The problem is how to get them to confide their senseless plans to you. You'll have to be subtle to coax out the full story. Once you have the facts you can react. However, don't jump the gun.

SATURDAY, 21ST NOVEMBER
Mercury retrograde

Mercury does one of its periodic turnabouts today, casting a web of misunderstandings between you and anyone who holds a special place in your affections. For the next four weeks you'll need to be crystal clear in all you say to avoid over-reactions or hostility from your partner. Keep your cool and be patient when talking over important issues.

SUNDAY, 22ND NOVEMBER
Sun into Sagittarius

The Sun moves into your Solar house of partnerships from today, so you'll be caught up in a romantic atmosphere that will be difficult, if not impossible, to resist. If you are married or involved in a close relationship this influence will tend to deepen your commitment and add to your happiness. If you're single, the next few weeks could see that special someone entering your life.

MONDAY, 23RD NOVEMBER
Venus conjunct Pluto

There is no doubt about it, you are going through a really important time as far as personal relationships are concerned. This could be the time when you and your lover decide to turn what you have into a permanent arrangement. Even if you are alone and have no interest in getting together with anyone, someone or something could change your mind today.

TUESDAY, 24TH NOVEMBER
Moon sextile Sun

You'll have a longing for far-off, exotic places, but going on your own won't be much fun. You need someone around you to share an adventure now. However, if you are on your own, go anyway. You'll find someone to be with when you get to wherever you're going!

WEDNESDAY, 25TH NOVEMBER
Venus sextile Uranus

Foreign affairs are likely to provide the highlights of the day. By that, we mean anything from an entertaining night out in an exotic restaurant to an affair with a foreigner! You'll please yourself on a day when the most unlikely event could lead to a romantic interlude.

THURSDAY, 26TH NOVEMBER
Moon sextile Saturn

This is a good day to set about a long-term project, especially if there's an educational slant to it. Therefore, start a course of training or research a new area of interest. You can ask friends for help if necessary, because they will be in the mood to give you just the information you need.

FRIDAY, 27TH NOVEMBER
Neptune into Aquarius

Your philosophical and religious leanings are emphasized by Neptune's entry into your ninth Solar house of beliefs. Neptune inspires your mind, leading you to higher levels of perception and a yearning for wisdom.

SATURDAY, 28TH NOVEMBER
Mars trine Neptune

Whether you are at home or at work today, you will find the world a good place and the people in it easy to get along with. Females could fall deeply and sincerely in love, while males could have the kind of romantic day that will be hard to forget. Dreams could come true, and whether you are looking for success on the sports field or for the job of a lifetime, go all out for it now.

SUNDAY, 29TH NOVEMBER
Sun conjunct Pluto

You'll feel in control today. In all dealings with others you'll be calling the shots and organizing the routine. You won't be afraid of forcing change either, so the cautious had better watch out! This new masterful you could be very attractive.

GEMINI

MONDAY, 30TH NOVEMBER
Moon conjunct Saturn

Now you will really find out who your friends are, because you will have the strength to confront anyone whom you suspect has been less than true. There may be some really good news concerning older relatives or people in positions of authority. You could also have a good time if involved in a group activity.

December at a Glance

LOVE	❤	❤		
WORK	★	★		
MONEY	£	£	£	
HEALTH	✚	✚	✚	✚
LUCK	⊔	⊔		

TUESDAY, 1ST DECEMBER
Mercury sextile Uranus

Be brave today and act on opportunity as it arises. You may get the chance to drop everything and rush off on a holiday with a loved one. If that's the case, you are likely to get a good deal with a travel firm. Mercury and Uranus ensure that this will be a day to remember!

WEDNESDAY, 2ND DECEMBER
Sun sextile Uranus

You could fall in love with a fascinating stranger today! Even if you don't actually go that far, you will certainly be attracted to someone new and they will be equally drawn to you. Enjoy this flirtatious mood for what it is and be careful not to get into trouble – unless you want to, of course. You may feel restless and in need of freedom.

THURSDAY, 3RD DECEMBER
Full Moon

You are rapidly coming to a decision about a particular partnership. Perhaps a previously harmonious situation is now becoming tense and fraught, or maybe you have outgrown a friendship. You seem to be looking for something different from the people around you, and this may affect the type of people with whom you choose to surround yourself.

FRIDAY, 4TH DECEMBER
Moon opposite Venus

Your own interests must take a back seat today because your other half is in dire need of some tender loving care and attention. Get your priorities right and all will be well. There's nothing so vital that can't be put off until another day, so devote some time to the one who means the most to you. Even if you're single, there's a friend in need close at hand.

SATURDAY, 5TH DECEMBER
Mercury sextile Mars

A wild and passionate affair is foretold by today's hot and steamy aspect between Mercury and Mars. Love may be the last thing on your mind, but Cupid's arrow is in full flight; you'll have no choice but to go along with it!

SUNDAY, 6TH DECEMBER
Moon trine Jupiter

You'll intuitively feel that there's a financial problem afoot that needs some serious thought. There's a chance to sort out what you should do in both your job and money matters now. Keep following your hunches and you'll discover a remarkable opportunity.

MONDAY, 7TH DECEMBER
Moon sextile Mars

You and your lover seem to have the same kind of values and priorities and there should be little friction between you. You may both be keen to do what you can for children, younger relatives or for other young people in your circle.

TUESDAY, 8TH DECEMBER
Moon trine Sun

The atmosphere around you should be all sweetness and light today. You are in a good mood and so are your nearest and dearest. Friends and relatives will be in touch for a good old gossip and, later on in the day, you and your partner will have a great time telling each other the day's news. You seem to be at home with yourself and any recent feelings of self-doubt will vanish.

WEDNESDAY, 9TH DECEMBER
Venus trine Saturn

Commitment, either to a person or an ideal, is the main issue today. You'll be determined to give your time, efforts or even the remainder of your life to something or someone very important. For once the heart dominates the head, but in this case it's no bad thing.

THURSDAY, 10TH DECEMBER
Moon square Sun

You'll become aware of disquieting undercurrents in both your family relations and with your partner today. It's obvious that there are some deep-seated complaints that no one has been willing to voice, and it's high time these were brought out into the open. Envy and resentment are issues that need to be tackled now if you want to restore harmony in your home.

FRIDAY, 11TH DECEMBER
Venus into Capricorn

You may feel slightly awkward and possessive over the next month or so, but outwardly at least you'll endeavour to keep the peace. This could be a good strategy, but you will probably need to dig in your heels at some point to show everyone concerned you mean business.

SATURDAY, 12TH DECEMBER
Mars sextile Pluto

Your emotions will guide you today, overruling your logic at every turn. Ignore the objections of everyone else and do as your feelings bid. You can't go wrong, and you could transform your life in an extremely positive way!

SUNDAY, 13TH DECEMBER
Moon sextile Sun

This is a time for togetherness and romance. The two great luminaries, the Sun and Moon, cast a golden light on affairs of the heart and promise a pleasurable interlude away from the hustle and bustle of daily life.

MONDAY, 14TH DECEMBER
Moon sextile Venus

It's a day of relaxation, but not necessarily calm. The Lunar aspect of Venus puts you in a sensual mood, determined to enjoy the finer things of life. Good food, good wine and the company of someone you love will be the perfect recipe for bliss. It doesn't matter what you do as long as you enjoy it.

GEMINI

TUESDAY, 15TH DECEMBER
Mars trine Uranus

Forget duty and go with the flow today. If there's a chance of a journey in congenial company, then go at once. The destination or the distance won't matter much because you're bound to have a whale of a time!

WEDNESDAY, 16TH DECEMBER
Moon sextile Neptune

You will find that you are easily influenced by the views and actions of others today, and will be quite prepared to follow their lead especially in work and monetary dealings.

THURSDAY, 17TH DECEMBER
Moon sextile Uranus

This suggestion may sound completely crazy, but you should consider visiting your in-laws today! If you can't visit them, then give them a ring to see how they are. You'll enjoy their company, and even if it's simply a duty visit you'll feel all the better for it. Your partner could spring a pleasant surprise on you later in the day.

FRIDAY, 18TH DECEMBER
New Moon

Just go on in the same way as usual and don't deny yourself anything! As far as today is concerned, the New Moon suggests that you take a fresh look at your partnerships and relationships, whether personal or professional.

SATURDAY, 19TH DECEMBER
Sun trine Saturn

Common sense rules the day, but you are unlikely to come up with any. Let other people do the planning, and be content to follow their line of reasoning. Don't allow personal pride to interfere with practicality.

SUNDAY, 20TH DECEMBER
Moon square Mars

Guard against silly accidents today. Don't allow your mind to wander while you are in charge of machinery or, worse still, while driving a vehicle. Something may break down, requiring specialist help in getting it fixed, or you may have to face the fact that an appliance has just about had its day and needs replacing.

GEMINI

MONDAY, 21ST DECEMBER
Mercury conjunct Pluto

You or your partner will have bees in your bonnets and won't rest until you've both had your say. Today's influence indicates a clearing of the air, so it's time to talk openly.

TUESDAY, 22ND DECEMBER
Sun into Capricorn

A highly passionate phase in your life begins with the Sun's entry into your area of sexuality, shared resources and physical attraction. You'll get further now if you are direct and to the point. Any intimate problem that has plagued you should be discussed with someone you trust to relieve anxieties. Your financial fortunes should also improve within the next month. A windfall is indicated for many; for others a more sensible use of cash resources will bring a greater return on investments.

WEDNESDAY, 23RD DECEMBER
Mercury sextile Uranus

It's likely to be a day of good news as the influence of Mercury and Uranus brings glad tidings from an official or legal source, or from overseas. Sudden journeys or unexpected visitors will pleasantly surprise you.

THURSDAY, 24TH DECEMBER
Moon square Pluto

There could be a conflict between your personal relationship and your career now. For example, your hours of work may mean that you only manage to communicate with each other by leaving notes on the kitchen table, and it may be hard to cope with the twin demands of home and working life. A rather vengeful woman could also interfere in your plans. If so, try to retain some Christmas spirit!

FRIDAY, 25TH DECEMBER
Moon conjunct Jupiter

This should be a very lucky Christmas Day. Your charm will win friends in high places, and past efforts will not go unrewarded as the Moon conjuncts Jupiter. Of course it's important not to exaggerate about your abilities or to deny past errors. If you can avoid these pitfalls, this should be a day of fortunate advancement.

SATURDAY, 26TH DECEMBER
Moon square Sun

You'll need some peace and quiet to sort out complex paperwork today, so you won't be keen on people dropping in unannounced! Being polite can sometimes be a strain, so stop dropping veiled hints and just tell them to push off!

SUNDAY, 27TH DECEMBER
Moon square Venus

Your mood is romantic and the stage could be set for a wonderfully loving day. However, someone could set out to spoil things completely, leaving you feeling thoroughly let down. If you and your lover plan to spend a peaceful day together, it's best to keep this information to yourselves rather than risk being disturbed by a sourpuss or jealous outsider.

MONDAY, 28TH DECEMBER
Mercury sextile Mars

You're in the mood for fun, and all it takes is a little persuasion to encourage a close friend or partner to join you. You may have something to celebrate and you'll be determined to have a riotous time if at all possible.

TUESDAY, 29TH DECEMBER
Saturn direct

The large, distant and rather gloomy planet Saturn turns to direct motion today, ending a rather tricky and boring phase. You may have had to do without your usual friends and acquaintances over the past few weeks, but they will soon be back to give you the help and support you need. If you have been involved in difficult dealings with an official of some kind, this too will soon be resolved.

WEDNESDAY, 30TH DECEMBER
Moon trine Neptune

There will be a wonderfully romantic feeling to the day today and this could lead to a pleasant flirtation or two with the most unlikely of people. You may hear good news from faraway relatives, perhaps leading to an invitation to visit them. If you have any legal worries, a rather strange and mysterious event could make your problems disappear.

THURSDAY, 31ST DECEMBER
Moon trine Mars

This should be an action-packed day! You'll be whizzing around trying to get a million and one things done in a very short time. Family duties are ever-present, although you have commitments elsewhere too. Of course all this pressure could make you difficult to deal with, and almost impossible to live with, so spare a thought for those long-suffering souls who have to cope with you. Apart from that, a very Happy New Year!

1999

January at a Glance

LOVE	❤	❤	❤	❤	❤
WORK	★	★	★	★	★
MONEY	£	£	£		
HEALTH	✚				
LUCK	♰	♰			

FRIDAY, 1ST JANUARY
Mercury square Jupiter

You should get a clue that someone very close isn't pursuing the wisest course at the start of this New Year. The problem is how to get them to open up to confide their senseless plans to you. You have to be subtle with this one and slowly coax the full story out. Once you have the facts you can react. However, don't jump the gun.

SATURDAY, 2ND JANUARY
Full Moon

Today's full Moon seems to be highlighting a minor problem in connection with financial matters today. You may have been overspending recently and this could be the cause of your current financial embarrassment but there does seem to be something deeper to be considered here. Perhaps the firm you work for has a temporary problem or maybe your partner is a bit short of cash just now.

SUNDAY, 3RD JANUARY
Moon opposite Venus

You may want to be the last of the big spenders today but it is not really a good idea. You may need to consult an accountant or your bank manager in order to see what you can or cannot get away with during the months ahead. There is no doubt about it, whether you have only yourself to answer to or whether you are part of any kind of partnership, you will have to cut down on the luxuries for a while.

MONDAY, 4TH JANUARY
Venus into Aquarius

Venus enters your Solar ninth house of exploration this month and this may make you slightly restless. Venus is concerned with the pleasures of life and also with leisure activities of all kinds, so explore such ideas as your sporting interests or perhaps of listening to interesting music or going to art galleries and the like. You may want to travel somewhere new and interesting soon.

TUESDAY, 5TH JANUARY
Venus conjunct Neptune

A quiet and sensitive day in which you can express some of those feelings that aren't easily put into words. The conjunction of Venus and Neptune gives you and your partner an instinctive understanding of each other's deepest thoughts, emotions and needs. Those who are unattached may find a soulmate today, someone who seems to provide a missing part to your life. One word of warning: any new relationship begun now may not last, since Neptune is also a planet of illusion. Ask yourself if you are only seeing what you want to see.

WEDNESDAY, 6TH JANUARY
Moon square Pluto

You will find it hard to cope with all the many and varied demands that are being placed on you at the moment. Your partner wants one thing, your family another and your job is also trying to claim a portion of your attention. You may feel like hiding away and forgetting the world for a while but you probably won't be able to get away with this. You could, if you are careful, manipulate things to suit you better.

THURSDAY, 7TH JANUARY
Mercury into Capricorn

Mercury moves into one of the most sensitive areas of your chart from today. Anything of an intimate nature from your physical relationships to the state of your bank balance comes under scrutiny now. Turn your heightened perceptions to your love life, important partnerships, and any affair that deals with investment, insurance, tax or shared resources. An intelligent approach now will save you a lot of problems later.

FRIDAY, 8TH JANUARY
Moon trine Venus

This is not a day for duty. The Lunar aspect to Venus puts a romantic spark in your soul. There's nothing you'd like better than an intimate *tête-à-tête* with someone you love. Forget your worries for today at least and take that special person in your life out for a night of glamour. If you haven't got a special person, go for glamour anyway. Someone will catch your eye.

SATURDAY, 9TH JANUARY
Moon square Sun

Personal desires and the expectations of others will tend to clash under the stressful aspect of the Moon and Sun. Accounts, contracts and paperwork have to be dealt with before you can take any time off.

SUNDAY, 10TH JANUARY
Moon opposite Saturn

You may find yourself out of sympathy with other members of the family who belong to different generations. It may be your parents or your in-laws who get you down today or it may be the children who are being impossible. There is very little opportunity for escape and freedom seems as far away as it does for a 'lifer' sitting in his lonely cell. You are not lonely enough, and that is the problem, really.

MONDAY, 11TH JANUARY
Moon square Uranus

Your confidence could slide down a dark hole today, leaving you wondering why you act so foolishly from time to time. You will begin to think that all your beliefs and ideas are wrong and that everyone else is cleverer than you. Worse still, this 'downer' mood could affect your ability to work and it could cause you to make mistakes which seem to emphasize your feelings of low-self esteem. This is just a phase and you should try not to let it get you down. Blame it on the planets.

TUESDAY, 12TH JANUARY
Venus sextile Pluto

You are in a mood to travel and to relax with your partner now, so if you can get away on a holiday, this would be an ideal time to do so. You may be equally keen to explore religious or philosophical ideas now, but Venus suggests that you would want to do this in good company and accompanied by good food and a drink or two.

WEDNESDAY, 13TH JANUARY
Venus conjunct Uranus

You should receive an invitation to some kind of celebration today. A friend may be getting married, a relative may have a new baby to show off or someone close to you may have a new home to celebrate. You may decide to take a trip over water soon and, if so, this would be quite luxurious and rather pleasant. You may also enjoy a good old discussion about religion or philosophy now.

THURSDAY, 14TH JANUARY
Sun sextile Jupiter

The fortunate influence of Jupiter is activated by the Sun today. All career affairs will go well, money should come in more readily and your sexual charisma should be on an all-time high. You can't go wrong!

FRIDAY, 15TH JANUARY
Sun square Mars

You could find yourself at loggerheads with others today. Children and young people in particular could get you down now. A lover may be in a jealous or destructive mood or you yourself may make a mess of things as a result of envy or unfounded suspicions.

SATURDAY, 16TH JANUARY
Moon conjunct Mercury

A declaration of love is certain today as the Moon conjuncts Mercury in your house of passion. This could be the start of something truly spectacular in your love life. You'll be able to talk freely about the most intimate needs and desires now. There's no room for embarrassment when there's such a harmony between two people.

SUNDAY, 17TH JANUARY
New Moon

Apart from a new Moon today, there are no major planetary happenings. This suggests that you avoid making major changes in your life just now but make a couple of fresh starts in very minor matters. You may feel like taking your partner to task over his or her irritating ways, but perhaps today is not the best day for doing this.

MONDAY, 18TH JANUARY
Sun square Saturn

Take care over any legal dealings today and, if you have to deal with the police or with any kind of government official today, then be patient and try to avoid getting on the wrong side of them. Someone may try to undermine your position in life and to make you feel small in some way. Try to rise above this kind of spiteful or humiliating behaviour and keep faith with yourself.

TUESDAY, 19TH JANUARY
Moon conjunct Venus

Today's stars promise nothing but harmony and contentment. The Moon makes a splendid contact with Venus this Friday and bestows the ability to enjoy life to its fullest. Any past family difficulties, such as rows with in-laws can now be put behind you and oil poured on troubled waters. You'll feel at one with the world.

WEDNESDAY, 20TH JANUARY
Sun into Aquarius

The Sun moves into your Solar ninth house today and it will stay there for a month. This would be a good time to travel overseas or to explore new neighbourhoods. It is also a good time to take up an interest in spiritual matters. You may find yourself keen to read about religious or philosophical subjects or even to explore the world of psychic healing over the next month or so.

THURSDAY, 21ST JANUARY
Mars opposite Saturn

One can't expect an easy day when Mars opposes Saturn, and when this unfortunate combination occurs in areas associated with leisure and friendships, one can't really expect these to go smoothly either. Frayed tempers and irritable people will be far too common today.

FRIDAY, 22ND JANUARY
Sun conjunct Neptune

Neptune will open your mind in ways that you cannot even begin to understand. You may be overwhelmed by some form of divine inspiration or, alternatively, you could find yourself opening up to an almost frightening level of psychic awareness. Don't be afraid, this is all meant to be, and it will show you how to make the best of yourself and your life and whom you can trust.

SATURDAY, 23RD JANUARY
Mercury sextile Jupiter

Good news is on its way. Probably this is about money so many will receive a cash gift or a windfall. The ambitious will do very well indeed because a promotion or new job is likely.

SUNDAY, 24TH JANUARY
Mercury square Saturn

If you come up against government officials or any other kind of authority figure today, be sure to co-operate with them totally and not to get their backs up. If you are given a parking ticket, so be it. If you feel that this is unfair, then write to the relevant department and explain yourself rather than trying to take it up with the traffic warden or the police officer who is at the scene.

MONDAY, 25TH JANUARY
Moon square Uranus

There may be a sudden event which makes you doubt your own sanity today. There is nothing wrong with your judgement, it is simply that everything is a bit off-centre just now. You may receive an unexpected call or letter from someone whom you had almost forgotten and this could stir memories which you had more or less forgotten. You may want to get away for a half-hour alone, so that you can think thighs over.

TUESDAY, 26TH JANUARY
Mars into Scorpio

The transit of Mars into your area of health and work shows that you must show that you have initiative and drive to make the most of your prospects now. The energies of the fiery planet won't allow you to sink anonymously into a crowd. You'll be forced to stand out and make your mark on the professional world. In health affairs, the vitality of the planet must be good news. Rarely have you felt so alive and effective. You may find that some colleagues are distressed at this assertion of your personality and aims. Unfortunately for them, they'll just have to put up with it!

WEDNESDAY, 27TH JANUARY
Venus sextile Saturn

An excursion with an older friend to something cultural and fun would do you the world of good today. You might have to be persuaded to leave your comfortable home, yet the outing will lift your spirits so give in and go!

THURSDAY, 28TH JANUARY
Venus into Pisces

Venus moves into your Solar house of ambition and prominence from today. If you're involved in any career in the arts, beautification, entertainment or public relations, then you're bound to do well over the next few weeks. Those who work for women bosses won't do badly either since a female influence in the workplace will aid your ambitions. Since Venus is the planet of charisma use diplomacy to solve professional problems. You can hardly fail to win with such a capacity for charm.

FRIDAY, 29TH JANUARY
Venus trine Mars

You're seeing your professional world in a different, more positive light today. You are now aware of the fortunate possibilities that await you in the future. This renewed vision inspires you to get on with the daily routine with vigour. It's far easier to tackle your chores when there's something to work for isn't it?

SATURDAY, 30TH JANUARY
Sun sextile Pluto

A longing for the far-off and exotic is strong today triggered by the aspect between the Sun and Pluto. You may feel the urge for travel to out-of-the-way places with strange-sounding names. The more mysterious and alluring the better.

SUNDAY, 31ST JANUARY
Full Moon eclipse

Today's eclipse signals impatience and restlessness as you examine many aspects of your life and find them wanting. It may be that you desire a house move away from a neighbourhood that is too familiar and stifling. You have a longing to expand your mental horizons and will wish to travel far and wide soaking up variety and new experiences. Since the effects of an eclipse can be felt up to three months after the event, your chance to move freely will come about within that time.

February at a Glance

LOVE	❤				
WORK	★	★	★	★	★
MONEY	£				
HEALTH	✛	✛	✛		
LUCK	U	U	U	U	

GEMINI

MONDAY, 1ST FEBRUARY
Mars square Neptune

It is hard to make sense of anybody or anything today because what they are telling you doesn't match up with what you know about the situation or with what your gut feeling is saying. A young man may be very charming and plausible now, but can he be believed? Probably not. It will be hard to get the chores done now because, just as you start to tackle one thing, something else needs attention.

TUESDAY, 2ND FEBRUARY
Sun conjunct Uranus

The Sun's conjunction with eccentric Uranus opens your eyes to the weird and wonderful possibilities that surround you. You will now see the world in a different light! An interest in a purely abstract subject could fascinate you. The stranger and more unique the topic the better! Your curiosity won't be satisfied with a mere library book now.

WEDNESDAY, 3RD FEBRUARY
Sun conjunct Mercury

If you have any kind of legal or official matter to deal with, this would be a good day to get on with it. It is a good time to sign contracts or agreements or to make a business deal. You seem to be taking a deep interest in spiritual matters now and this may be the start of something which will affect the course of your life from here on.

THURSDAY, 4TH FEBRUARY
Moon opposite Jupiter

It's too easy to get carried away with your own enthusiasm today. Your family too is full of big ideas which you should be trying to temper; unfortunately you are in too much of a state of high excitement to be realistic. With everyone egging the others on it's hard to get a grip on reality today. Don't underestimate the hard work needed to ground your dreams in reality.

FRIDAY, 5TH FEBRUARY
Mercury conjunct Uranus

It's an important day to talk through any radical plans and far-out schemes with your partner. If you keep everything to yourself, you'll be thought to be eccentric at best, downright weird at worst. You may be open to new and exciting ideas, but your partner may be of a more conservative frame of mind. Take time to explain your actions and intentions now.

SATURDAY, 6TH FEBRUARY
Venus square Pluto

Watch out for sexual harassment at your place of work today. If someone says or does something objectionable, then tell them so. Don't let them get away with this, because they will only think that they have a licence to continue with their unkind behaviour. Guard against being manipulated by others now, keep a clear eye on your own goals and don't allow others to deflect you from these.

SUNDAY, 7TH FEBRUARY
Moon conjunct Mars

It's a highly energetic and vital day as the Moon conjuncts Mars. It's fast and furious action all the way but at least you've got the physical strength and tenacity to cope with the pressure. In work, if you can keep your head while all around you are losing theirs, you won't be doing too badly at all.

MONDAY, 8TH FEBRUARY
Moon square Sun

You may find it hard to concentrate on your usual chores today because other things seem to be intruding on your mind. It would be nice just to sit and dream or to stand gazing out of the window for an hour or so, but the chances are that you won't be able to do any of this. Your mind is full of interesting philosophical thoughts and ideas but the work also needs to be done.

TUESDAY, 9TH FEBRUARY
Moon trine Jupiter

After some of pressures you've been under, careerwise and in terms of burning the candle at both ends, it's time you looked at the state your physique is getting into. The Moon's aspect to Jupiter points out the benefits of a new health regime. This is a good day to work out with some aerobics, or if that's too energetic, moderate your intake with a new diet. Look after yourself.

WEDNESDAY, 10TH FEBRUARY
Moon sextile Uranus

There could be some really unexpected news from overseas or from someone who is at a distance from you now. Fortunately, the news is good and this will allay any fears that you may have had about your distant friend or relative's health and welfare. For some of you, love could come sweeping into your life and it could be a fascinating foreigner or someone from a different culture who makes your heart pound so.

THURSDAY, 11TH FEBRUARY
Mercury sextile Saturn

You may find yourself saying goodbye to an old friend today, but this should not cause you any great concern. This person will turn up again before long and the pleasure of your reunion will more than make up for the separation that you have endured.

FRIDAY, 12TH FEBRUARY
Mercury into Pisces

There's a certain flexibility entering your career structure as indicated by the presence of Mercury in your Solar area of ambition from today. You can now turn your acute mind to all sorts of career problems and solve them to everyone's satisfaction, and your own personal advantage. Your powers of persuasion will be heightened from now on, ensuring that you charm bosses and employers to get your own way. Those seeking work should attend interviews because their personality will shine.

SATURDAY, 13TH FEBRUARY
Jupiter into Aries

The trials and tribulations of the past few months are fading away rapidly now and you can begin to enjoy the lighter side of life once again. Your sense of humour will come bubbling back up the surface again and there will soon be plenty for you to laugh and joke about. Your best bet is to keep yourself in the swim by joining clubs, societies or groups of people who share your interests.

SUNDAY, 14TH FEBRUARY
Moon sextile Jupiter

If a friend suggests a short holiday, weekend break or just a jaunt to your local shopping centre, you should immediately accept. This is your chance to have a lot of fun and encounter some new faces. The more intellectually inclined will benefit too since your interest is bound to be stimulated in social settings.

MONDAY, 15TH FEBRUARY
Moon conjunct Uranus

An unexpected invitation from a distant friend will ensure that you are soon packing your bags and making travel arrangements. If you travel within the next month and if you are unattached, a holiday romance or even something further reaching than this could set your heart beating wildly! Alternatively, unexpected visitors from distant locations might soon descend upon you and this could lead to an unexpected romantic adventure.

GEMINI

TUESDAY, 16TH FEBRUARY
New Moon eclipse

The eclipse in your area of travel will provide more than a few hitches to your plans. Check over all arrangements for journeys extra carefully today. Let caution be your watchword and don't let impatience rule your life.

WEDNESDAY, 17TH FEBRUARY
Sun sextile Saturn

You have a fine grasp of the finer points of human interaction today, and can analyse any and all issues that are troubling certain friends. Your common sense, combined with a sprinkling of charisma can show them the error of their ways and provide relief from anxieties.

THURSDAY, 18TH FEBRUARY
Mercury square Pluto

There seems to be a heavy and stressful emphasis on your ambitions just now and it seems that your personal relationships are in conflict with these. You may find that your partner is not in sympathy with what you are trying to achieve, or that he or she considers that their needs come before your objectives. Try talking this over with your other half and, if this doesn't work, try getting some kind of independent counsellor to help.

FRIDAY, 19TH FEBRUARY
Sun into Pisces

The Sun moves decisively into your horoscope area of ambition from today bringing in a month when your worldly progress will achieve absolute priority. You need to feel that what you are doing is worthwhile and has more meaning than simply paying the bills. You may feel the urge to change you career, to make a long-term commitment to a worthwhile cause, or simply to demand recognition for past efforts. However this ambitious phase manifests you can be sure that your prospects are considerably boosted from now on.

SATURDAY, 20TH FEBRUARY
Void Moon

This is one of those days when none of the planets are making any worthwhile kind of aspect to any of the others. Even the Moon is 'void of course', which means that it is not making any aspects of any importance to any of the other planets. On such a day, avoid starting anything new and don't set out to do anything important. Do what needs to be done and take some time off for a rest.

SUNDAY, 21ST FEBRUARY
Venus into Aries

Venus moves into your eleventh house of friendship and group activities today, bringing a few weeks of happiness and harmony for you and your friends. You could fall in love under this transit or you could reaffirm your feelings towards a current partner. You should be looking and feeling rather good now but, if not, this is a good time to spend some money on your appearance and also to do something about any nagging health problems.

MONDAY, 22ND FEBRUARY
Venus sextile Neptune

This should be a really happy day in which you can enjoy the company of friends and family alike. You may find yourself entertaining a fascinating stranger but you could just as easily find that such a person takes you out to dinner and entertains you in style! Foreigners and unusual people may make some kind of interesting and important contribution to your life now and some of you could fall in love with one of these now.

TUESDAY, 23RD FEBRUARY
Moon opposite Pluto

Today has got more than its fair share of problems, yet with a methodical attitude and a little determination you'll work your way through them all. There's a conflict between duty and pleasure now, and for once duty seems to come out on top. A difficult task may have to be finished before you can allow yourself quality time. If that's the case, then get on with it, the sooner started, the sooner finished. A friend may also need you as a shoulder to cry on.

WEDNESDAY, 24TH FEBRUARY
Venus conjunct Jupiter

You will be in the mood to take risks today and, for the most part, these will come off. Some of you could fall hopelessly in love today, but the attraction is so sudden and so overwhelming that it will be hard to keep it going for long on such an intense level. Nevertheless, this could be a memorable event and even those of you who are happily settled with a partner may still feel drawn to someone else today.

THURSDAY, 25TH FEBRUARY
Moon trine Sun

At last that terrible restlessness is under control. As the Moon harmoniously links with the Sun a contentment and calmness overtakes your mood. You'll feel as if you're getting somewhere, and that the next stages are obvious. This happier atmosphere may have something to do with a small financial boost that should turn up very soon.

FRIDAY, 26TH FEBRUARY
Sun trine Mars

You'll be so businesslike today that even the most difficult of tasks will be tackled with ease. You've got a lot of energy at your disposal. Combine that with a competitive urge and you're bound to be on a winner.

SATURDAY, 27TH FEBRUARY
Jupiter sextile Neptune

This should be an enjoyable day and you may go on a journey to meet up with some friends. An outing to an art gallery, concert, musical event or just the cinema would be a favoured activity today.

SUNDAY, 28TH FEBRUARY
Moon opposite Uranus

You'll feel that your partner is irritable and perverse today, but if you asked them, they'd say it was you! I think the problem here is one of communication. Are there worries and major issues that are not being discussed in your household? If that's the case, then you should put it right at once. There may be a confrontation, but at least it will clear the air and put your relationship back on a more reasonable basis.

March at a Glance

LOVE	❤	❤	❤	❤
WORK	★	★	★	★
MONEY	£			
HEALTH	✪	✪		
LUCK	♨	♨		

GEMINI

MONDAY, 1ST MARCH
Saturn into Taurus

The influence of Saturn moves into your twelfth house of secrets and psychology from today. This brings the lesson that you've got to stand on your own feet and be totally self-reliant. You will tend to feel the need to isolate yourself for a while and get to grips with some difficult questions that have been bothering you.

TUESDAY, 2ND MARCH
Mercury into Aries

The swift-moving planet Mercury enters your eleventh Solar house today and gives a remarkable uplift to your social prospects. During the next few weeks you'll find yourself at the centre point of friendly interactions. People will seek you out for the pleasure of your company. It's also a good time to get in contact with distant friends and those you haven't seen for a while. The only fly in the ointment is that you shouldn't expect a small phone bill.

WEDNESDAY, 3RD MARCH
Venus trine Pluto

If you're involved in an affair that has been fun, but without any deep commitment, you could find that situation changing now. A more powerful bond is required by one or other of you. How the other party responds will make or break the relationship. If you are alone, then a meeting could rapidly alter that state. A deepening passion is the hallmark of the day.

THURSDAY, 4TH MARCH
Venus sextile Uranus

Today's fun-loving aspect between Venus and Uranus shows that this is no time for mundane duties of any kind. Novelty is the thing, and if you're romantically inclined, variety and a little flirtation are the spices of life. Those married or otherwise attached should take the stellar hint and put some of the magic back into your relationship. Do something different, either singly or with a close companion today.

FRIDAY, 5TH MARCH
Mercury sextile Neptune

There's some surprising news in the offing, and you and a partner will be confused or unsure of your response. When in doubt do nothing and await developments. It's more than likely that the message has got garbled in transmission so it's too soon to react. Don't listen to gossip because it's likely to be inaccurate. The true situation is far less worrying than today's information would suggest.

SATURDAY, 6TH MARCH
Moon square Neptune

It's obvious that you're on a see-saw of energy at the moment. You tend to be unaccountably tired today, and not quite with it as far as your duties are concerned. Take it easy, you've been through a lot recently and could do with a break. However, there may be just one job that you have to do before you can relax completely today.

SUNDAY, 7TH MARCH
Moon square Uranus

Your mind will be so active that any attempt to tie you down to mundane duty will be severely resented today. You'd like to make a break for freedom but obligations weigh heavily on your shoulders.

MONDAY, 8TH MARCH
Moon trine Venus

Things are looking up now! Those of you who are alone and lonely would do well to get out and about today, because there is definitely something in the air. A friend may introduce you to a potential mate or you may make new friends now who may turn into lovers at a later date. Those of you who are happily settled will enjoy the company of your partner and also of good friends later on today.

TUESDAY, 9TH MARCH
Moon trine Jupiter

If you and your lover get together with friends, you will find that a chat will do much to cheer you both up and also to clear your minds about one or two points. A visit to your local hostelry might be just the place for this. There should be good news about money matters coming your way today and the results of this will be shared between you and your lover.

WEDNESDAY, 10TH MARCH
Mercury retrograde

Today begins a period when your optimism will fall short of its usual level. It's the fault of Mercury which turns retrograde. This isn't a serious problem but you must be aware that at times you will feel as if your hopes have been dashed and your faith in friends misplaced. Of course there's little substance in these feelings yet rumours in the next few weeks may be disturbing.

GEMINI

THURSDAY, 11TH MARCH
Moon square Mercury

It's a very confusing day on most fronts when your mental processes are slowed down and clouded by the Moon's influence. Red tape, documents, and official correspondence will leave you paralysed with indecision. All you want to do is escape and possibly ask a friend to help out; unfortunately that won't do much good, since friends are as confused as you are. This is not a good day to deal with far-reaching business or financial affairs anyway so try to put them off.

FRIDAY, 12TH MARCH
Moon sextile Mars

Your work will take on an investigative quality today. You may need to find out what is going on in your workplace, even if only to catch up with the gossip. You may need to do some form of practical investigation, such as taking something to bits in order to find out why it isn't working properly. You may even decide to go to the doctor to discuss any worrying symptoms that you may have.

SATURDAY, 13TH MARCH
Mercury sextile Neptune

If you allow it to happen, you could be filled with joy and inspiration today. Friends and acquaintances will be ready to point you in the right direction and they may introduce you to ideas and methods which you would have never have considered if left to yourself. You could find your mind clear and sharp now but there is a slight problem in that you seem to insist on looking for the best in people, even when it doesn't exist.

SUNDAY, 14TH MARCH
Moon sextile Pluto

Your emotional state depends upon the behaviour of those who are around you today. Therefore, if your lover or your family are happy and co-operative, you will be happy, but if they are tense and restless, this will have a knock-on effect on your mood. You could do well to sort out any joint legal or official matters now, because these things will go smoothly and more quickly now than normal.

MONDAY, 15TH MARCH
Moon sextile Venus

The call of the new is very evident today since you'd do nearly anything just to have a change. You'd be off around the world like a shot if you could manage it. This scenario is unlikely just at the moment, but you can still inject a little of the exotic into your life even if it's only a Chinese meal!

TUESDAY, 16TH MARCH
Moon square Pluto

There could be a conflict between your personal relationship and your career now. For example, your hours of work may mean that you only manage to communicate with each other by leaving notes on the kitchen table. Or you may find it hard to cope with the twin demands of home and working life. There may be some interference in your plans which comes from the direction of a spiteful or vengeful woman.

WEDNESDAY, 17TH MARCH
New Moon

The new Moon today shows the great heights that you could possibly attain. The message is that there's nothing to fear except fear itself. Reach for the stars and you've got it made. Your career should begin to blossom now and you can achieve the kind of respect and status that you are looking for over the next month or so.

THURSDAY, 18TH MARCH
Venus into Taurus

As Venus enters your Solar house of secrets and psychology, it's obvious that the next few weeks will increase the importance of discretion in your romantic life. You'll find that it'll be wise to draw a veil over the more intimate side of your nature, and you'll be less inclined to confide your deepest secrets even to your closest friends. Quiet interludes with the one you love will be far more attractive than painting the town red just now.

FRIDAY, 19TH MARCH
Sun conjunct Mercury

A free and frank exchange of views is signalled by the conjunction of the Sun and Mercury. In all working situations, from a shop-floor conversation to the most high-powered executive meeting your views are important. Don't hold back. Raise objections to daft schemes, make sensible suggestions for better practices and more advantageous contracts. You can really do yourself some good by being assertive now. If you're unemployed, there couldn't be a better day to arrange or attend interviews.

SATURDAY, 20TH MARCH
Venus conjunct Saturn

It's obvious that you're preoccupied with your own big plans today, since those who are special to you think that you're being rather distant and cool. It's all the fault of Venus, whose now in to cool embrace of Saturn. It's not that your opinions or feelings have changed, it's just that you may have a little difficulty in expressing them freely now.

SUNDAY, 21ST MARCH
Sun into Aries

As the Sun makes its yearly entrance into your eleventh Solar house, you can be sure that friends and acquaintances are going to have a powerful influence on your prospects. The Sun's harmonious angle to your own sign gives an optimism and vitality to your outgoing nature. Social life will increase in importance over the next month. You'll be a popular and much sought-after person. Obstacles that have irritated you will now be swept away.

MONDAY, 22ND MARCH
Moon trine Neptune

You're obviously in an adventurous frame of mind today. The Moon and Neptune urge you to explore some obscure byways in the search for truth. Not only that, you'll be more than willing to provoke debate by taking an unconventional stance. Principles are the most important thing to you now, so being bogged down in mere practicalities isn't your scene at all.

TUESDAY, 23RD MARCH
Venus square Neptune

Though you can think of a million and one things to do to alleviate boredom, you probably can't get the energy together to do one of them. You may be prone to being overly romantic at the moment and the tendency to escape into amorous fantasy will overrule any hint of common sense today.

WEDNESDAY, 24TH MARCH
Moon square Sun

You are beginning to realize that one of your friends doesn't share your values. Perhaps your friend is the type who enjoys keeping you on the other end of the phone for hours on end while he or she has yet another good moan. If pointing out to your friend that your time is limited doesn't get you anywhere, you may have to give this particular pal the old heave-ho!

THURSDAY, 25TH MARCH
Sun sextile Neptune

New friends and acquaintances seem set to come sweeping into your life at a rate of knots now. You could find yourself meeting people who have the same outlook and philosophy of life as you do or, alternatively, you could find people who fascinate you because they are so different from you. Either way, today's events will fill you with inspiration and hope for the future in a way that you have never experienced before.

FRIDAY, 26TH MARCH
Moon square Saturn

You're likely to be in a despondent mood now. It's too easy to be pessimistic today, but you should remember that every cloud's got a sliver lining, and it's mainly a matter of your frame of mind. Console yourself with the thought that the general outlook is good, so do try to smile.

SATURDAY, 27TH MARCH
Venus opposite Mars

You will tend to experience some kind of inner conflict today as changing circumstances force you to make compromises. You may not be altogether happy about this since it will in some way go against your own sense of rightness.

SUNDAY, 28TH MARCH
Void Moon

Occasionally one finds a day in which neither the planets nor the Moon make any major aspects to each other and on such a day, the Moon's course is said to be 'void'. There is nothing wrong with a day like this but there is no point in trying to start anything new or anything important because there isn't enough of a planetary boost to get it off the ground. Stick to your normal routine.

MONDAY, 29TH MARCH
Moon square Pluto

With the Moon in square aspect to Pluto, there is some evidence that you will drop something important on the floor today, so make sure that you have a soapy cloth near by to mop up the spills! When out of the kitchen, you may find yourself being given news which is private or even secret. If so, there is good reason to respect the wishes of the person who gave the information by keeping it to yourself

TUESDAY, 30TH MARCH
Jupiter trine Pluto

The exuberant combination of Jupiter, planet of luck, and Pluto, the governor of hidden desires, shows that you are going to get what you want! It's rare that you can fulfil your desires to such an extent. Don't knock it!

WEDNESDAY, 31ST MARCH
Full Moon

Your creative soul and romantic yearnings come under the influence of today's Full Moon, so it's time to take stock of those things in your life that no longer give any emotional satisfaction. Children and younger people may need a word or two of advice now and the love lives of all around you will become the centre of interest. You're own romantic prospects may see an upturn too.

April at a Glance

LOVE	❤	❤	❤	❤
WORK	★	★	★	★
MONEY	£	£	£	£
HEALTH	✚	✚		
LUCK	U	U	U	

THURSDAY, 1ST APRIL
Sun conjunct Jupiter

This is a good day to go shopping because you will find just what you want and whatever you buy will be appreciated by those whom it is meant for. If you make plans for a holiday now, they will work out well. It is actually quite a good time to get away for a trip or an outing if you can do so. Your mood is happy and optimistic now.

FRIDAY, 2ND APRIL
Mercury direct

Mercury returns to direct motion from today and that should put a stop to all the setbacks, and disappointments that have bedevilled your career for the last few weeks. Suddenly, plans you'd put on the back burner are important again. Your path towards your aims will be much smoother than you expect. An ongoing dialogue with an employer or manager will be beneficial to your career prospects.

SATURDAY, 3RD APRIL
Moon conjunct Mars

If you are looking for love, then your workplace is one place where you may find it. Another potential place would be somewhere to do with health and healing. It would be crazy to expect to meet the love of your life in a hospital waiting room but funnier things have happened and fate can spring some really strange surprises. If you have all you love you need, then get the work done today.

SUNDAY, 4TH APRIL
Mercury sextile Venus

A private inspiration will be a source of comfort to you today. In career affairs your vision of what is possible may not be appreciated by those around you, but you know it to be true. Keep faith, because you will achieve it in the end.

MONDAY, 5TH APRIL
Moon sextile Neptune

There's quite a romantic outlook today. Anything done in company will be marvellous. A journey made with your partner or a close friend will be exceptionally enjoyable even if you don't actually converse. It'll be a case of enjoying each other's company on a more spiritual level.

TUESDAY, 6TH APRIL
Saturn square Neptune

Are you completely sure that you are being realistic enough? Saturn's aspect to Neptune urges a reassessment of your prospects. If you need to get away to think about important issues, then plan this now.

WEDNESDAY, 7TH APRIL
Sun sextile Uranus

The appeal of leaving your daily cares behind you is very strong today. The Sun makes contact with the restless planet Uranus, which sets your feet tapping with impatience to be up and away. Since this aspect is a good one you can expect the opportunity to escape the routine to occur now. For the very fortunate, a trip abroad is indicated. You need some novelty, and today should inject some into your life.

THURSDAY, 8TH APRIL
Moon sextile Mars

Keep alert for hints today because following up on a lead could considerably enhance your income. If you're back at work, you may get wind of a plot or arrangement behind closed doors that will have implications for the entire workforce. Don't jump to any conclusions though, because nothing is finalized as yet.

GEMINI

FRIDAY, 9TH APRIL
Moon sextile Mercury

Check out the rumours that are travelling around your workplace. There may be talk of mergers and takeovers and of hiring and firings. Some of these may only be rumours but other bits of information may have some truth in them. On a more personal level, this is a good time to get passionate with your partner and to enjoy your favourite and sexiest amusements.

SATURDAY, 10TH APRIL
Moon square Saturn

After your optimistic hopes, the reaction sets in today and you feel let down with a bump. You can see the obstacles in front of you too clearly now, but this is still not a reason for despondency. So there are some hurdles, you always knew that. Keep up the belief in yourself.

SUNDAY, 11TH APRIL
Moon sextile Sun

This is a great day of getting out and about, meeting up with friends and attending social gatherings of all kinds. You should have a pretty good time in company because this is not a day for solitary activity.

MONDAY, 12TH APRIL
Venus into Gemini

The luxury-loving planet, Venus, is suggesting that this is a great time to spoil yourself and also to enjoy yourself. So treat yourself to something nice and new that is for you alone. A new outfit would be a good idea or a few nice-smelling toiletries. Throw a party for your favourite friends and don't look the other way if someone seems to be fancying you.

TUESDAY, 13TH APRIL
Moon sextile Venus

There is an element of skulduggery going on at your place of work today, so don't make any major decisions or take much in the way of action until you know the strength of this. Away from work, the atmosphere is peaceful and charming and you can enjoy the company of friends, family and lovers in perfect harmony. Enjoy this oasis of pleasantness while it lasts because days like this are rare.

WEDNESDAY, 14TH APRIL
Moon into Aries

An original and innovative influence continues today when the Moon transits the house of ideals. You'll be stimulated by new ideas and will be anxious to meet with people who have a positive and possibly eccentric view of life.

THURSDAY, 15TH APRIL
Moon conjunct Jupiter

You may be on the receiving end of a windfall today. A friend may whisk you away to interesting places or there could be unexpected good luck of an unusual kind now. You may receive an invitation to travel to new and fascinating places or you may even win a holiday as a prize of some kind. As you can see, this is one of those truly red-letter days in which anything could happen.

FRIDAY, 16TH APRIL
New Moon

There's no doubt that issues surrounding friendship and trust are very important now. The New Moon in your horoscopic area of social activities ensures that encounters with interesting people will yield new and enduring friendships. Though your mood has tended to vary between optimism and despair recently, the new Moon can't fail to increase your confidence and vitality.

SATURDAY, 17TH APRIL
Mercury into Aries

Mercury will soon start to bring a remarkable uplift to your social prospects. Over the next few weeks, you'll find yourself at the centre point of friendly interactions. People will seek you out for the pleasure of your company. It's also a good time to get in contact with distant friends and those you haven't seen for a while. The only fly in the ointment is that you shouldn't expect a small phone bill.

SUNDAY, 18TH APRIL
Moon conjunct Venus

There are some wonderful opportunities around for you to improve your financial position now, but there are some equally good opportunities for finding a real bargain or for buying something that is going to stand the test of time. Romantically speaking, this should be a really comfortable day in which you and your lover snuggle up on the sofa and make an early start on the evening's entertainments!

MONDAY, 19TH APRIL
Mars opposite Saturn

Any overt pressure placed on you today will reflect on your health. You are particularly prone to stress at the moment and should try to trip down your schedule until you feel more up to the tasks in hand.

TUESDAY, 20TH APRIL
Sun into Taurus

The Sun moves into your house of secrets and psychology today making you very aware of your own inner world of dreams and imagination. For the next month you'll be very aware of the hurdles that face you, and all those things that tend to restrict your freedom; however your imagination and almost psychic insight will provide the necessary clues to overcome these obstacles. Issues of privacy are very important for the next few weeks.

WEDNESDAY, 21ST APRIL
Venus opposite Pluto

Venus's opposition to Pluto shows that change is imminent in close personal relationships. You may find that your heart lies elsewhere or that a deeper commitment is now required that will change the way you live your life. Your heart rules your head at the moment and you have little choice but to follow its dictates.

THURSDAY, 22ND APRIL
Mercury sextile Neptune

You will be completely in tune with both your surroundings and with your friends today. Your deep understanding of their inner workings could give you the reputation of being something of a psychic.

FRIDAY, 23RD APRIL
Jupiter sextile Uranus

The combination of Uranus and Jupiter shows that an impromptu trip is on the cards. Go on! Make a break for freedom. You know that you deserve some fun in different surroundings!

SATURDAY, 24TH APRIL
Sun opposite Mars

You may be feeling under the weather today. You can't quite put your finger on it, but there's something nagging away at the back of your mind and it's having a very negative effect on your well-being. There is the possibility that you're getting irritated with yourself and those around you. Others may seem obstructive and unhelpful but you must realize that you're projecting your insecurities onto them. Try to give yourself some space now.

GEMINI

SUNDAY, 25TH APRIL
Moon trine Saturn

If ever there was a day to stick close to your home patch, this is it! With the Moon and Saturn putting such an emphasis on privacy and comfort, you'd be doing yourself no favours if you strayed too far. Put your feet up and relax if you can possibly contain your impulsive nature. If not, then potter around catching up on all those neglected chores around the house.

MONDAY, 26TH APRIL
Mercury trine Pluto

You might have found it difficult to talk about the new directions and desires that have excited you recently, but today the aspect between Mercury and Pluto opens a channel of communication between yourself and a loved one.

TUESDAY, 27TH APRIL
Sun conjunct Saturn

It's getting more obvious that all your well-meaning intentions, and appreciation of your life's potential isn't cutting any ice with the grim practicalities of day-to-day existence. You've got to get down to detail and sort out some pressing matters before you can possibly create your ideal world. I know it's boring, yet very necessary if you're to make the most of the more expansive messages coming from your chart.

WEDNESDAY, 28TH APRIL
Moon opposite Mercury

Your mind may be set on having fun with your friends but try not to overload your already stretched schedule. Practical affairs have to be dealt with whether you're in the mood or not. I know you want to party but you'll only end up over-tired and edgy. It may be a case of all work and no play, but it's better in the long run. Resist friends who insist that you be sociable. That's only replacing one duty with another.

THURSDAY, 29TH APRIL
Mercury sextile Uranus

Literally anything could happen today! Two unconventional planets, Mercury and Uranus, unite to take you on a magical mystery tour, and who knows where you'll end up. Plan nothing because it's likely that you'll end up doing something else, somewhere else! At least it's going to be exciting!

FRIDAY, 30TH APRIL
Full Moon

Something is coming to a head in relation to your job. This is not a major crisis and there is absolutely no need to flounce out of a perfectly good job, but there is a problem that should be solved before you can continue on in a happy and peaceful frame of mind. You may have to sort out what your role is and which part of the job other people should be doing, because it looks as if you are carrying too much of the load at the moment.

May at a Glance

LOVE	♥	♥	♥		
WORK	★	★	★	★	★
MONEY	£	£	£	£	£
HEALTH	☉	☉	☉		
LUCK	⊍	⊍	⊍	⊍	

SATURDAY, 1ST MAY
Mercury conjunct Jupiter

Your mind is going at full pelt today and you could come up with some brilliant schemes. Make sure that these are practical as well as exciting and also guard against being talked into a get-rich-quick scheme by others. Focus your mind on your most important objective and get on with doing it now. Don't get side-tracked by time-wasting behaviour.

SUNDAY, 2ND MAY
Moon sextile Neptune

You can be such a softy sometimes! Today, your heart is worn on your sleeve and thoughts of love are never far from your mind. A partner may be surprised by the intensity of feeling you express now. However, you may be more interested in a cuddle rather than an erotic experience.

MONDAY, 3RD MAY
Moon sextile Uranus

Our suggestion may sound completely crazy but you should try paying a visit to your in-laws today! If you can't visit them, then give them a ring to see how they are. The chances are that if you went to see them you would enjoy their company, and even if this were simply a duty visit, you would feel better for having done your duty. Your partner will spring a pleasant surprise on you later in the day.

TUESDAY, 4TH MAY
Moon opposite Venus

Your loved ones may be in a tetchy mood today, so steer clear of domestic disputes and try to get your lover and the kids to relax. Should the season be chilly, it would be a good time to snuggle up in front of the fire, toast a few crumpets and open a bottle of something nice and warming. Get a pack of cards out or try your hands at a bit of Scrabble. Whatever the weather, concentrate on maintaining domestic harmony!

WEDNESDAY, 5TH MAY
Mars into Libra

Mars moves into a very creative area of your chart now, so if there is a project that you would like to get started upon, Mars will give you the drive and energy with which to do it. This is a good day for any kind of sporting or energetic pursuit so, if you want to practise your skills or get ready for some kind of future competition, then get down to it today.

THURSDAY, 6TH MAY
Moon square Jupiter

You may have to put yourself out on behalf of others today with friends being especially keen to have your help and energy on their side. Don't resent this kind of activity because it will bring some kind of karmic benefit later on when it will be your turn to call on your friends for their support. Your optimistic and positive outlook will help others to climb out of their melancholy moods.

FRIDAY, 7TH MAY
Neptune retrograde

The large, distant and slow-moving planet Neptune turns to retrograde motion today and this will bring a kind of slowing down in one or two areas of your life. Those of you who are studying are most likely to be affected by this planetary movement, while those who have long-term travel plans may find that they have to wait a while before getting away. You may find it hard to distinguish truth from fiction for a while.

SATURDAY, 8TH MAY
Mercury into Taurus

You'll find yourself in a more introspective mood for a few weeks because Mercury, planet of the mind, enters the most secret and inward-looking portion of your horoscope from today. This is the start of a period when you'll want to understand the inner being, your own desires and motivations. Too much hectic life will prove a distraction now so go by instinct and seek out solitude when you feel like it.

SUNDAY, 9TH MAY
Mercury sextile Venus

Though financially today's stars look good, there may be a nagging doubt about whether you are doing the right thing. A tasteful purchase may be just what you need, but are you sure that you can afford it?

MONDAY, 10TH MAY
Moon square Pluto

It is no good trying to throw your weight around today because this will not be appreciated by your superiors at work or by your loved ones at home. One of the reasons for your frustration is that it will be hard for you to reach even the most modest of your goals today. An older woman may irritate you or, worse still, you could simply sink into a strangely negative frame of mind for a while.

TUESDAY, 11TH MAY
Mercury square Neptune

It's important not to be too trusting at the moment. The planet Mercury, ruler of the mind, is under the deceptive influence of Neptune which shows that there is some deceit about. The worst thing is that it's probably a close friend or partner that is concealing the truth from you. Perhaps it isn't being done deliberately, but still it's not pleasant to harbour suspicions. It will take a while to sort out this complication, but resolve it you will.

WEDNESDAY, 12TH MAY
Moon trine Pluto

Children will take up much of your time today and you could learn a few surprising truths. It's about time that some of the childlike wonder was reintroduced into your life. And, if you can manage to see the world through a youngster's eyes, you'll be amazed that you'd forgotten what a truly marvellous place the universe is.

GEMINI

THURSDAY, 13TH MAY
Mercury conjunct Saturn

Secrets and confidences are the main theme of today's stars. If you're the one who finds that keeping up a cloak of concealment is a terrible strain on the nerves, then be prepared to share the dreadful facts with someone close. We think you'll find that it's not so dreadful after all, and will be surprised at the understanding you receive. They say that confession is good for the soul.

FRIDAY, 14TH MAY
Moon sextile Venus

If you can possibly manage to get away from the rat race today, it would be a marvellous idea. The Lunar aspect to Venus shows that your mind isn't on worldly duties at all now so you may as well relax that fevered brow and try to renew your energies by taking it easy. It doesn't matter what you do to pass the time as long as you enjoy yourself. Perhaps you should indulge in a little luxury, the treat would do you good.

SATURDAY, 15TH MAY
New Moon

The world of romance is especially attractive on a day when your dreams and fantasies take over your life. The New Moon points the way to new emotional experiences in the future, but you mustn't cling to the past because of misplaced loyalty or guilt. Some people are leaving your life, but if you were honest you'd admit that they're no real loss. Follow your instincts now and your dreams may well come true.

SUNDAY, 16TH MAY
Venus sextile Saturn

Today provides a splendid opportunity to show how sensible and shrewd you can be. You're business minded now and have the chance to make some considerable profit simply because you see an opening where others only see a blank wall. The aspect between Venus and Saturn is a very caring one though, so you're likely to spend your profits on someone else as soon as they've arrived.

MONDAY, 17TH MAY
Mercury square Uranus

Too much thinking can be bad for you! Especially when you dwell on old disappointments, hurt and failures. If you aren't careful, you'll persuade yourself that you are totally worthless. Nothing could be further from the truth!

GEMINI

TUESDAY, 18TH MAY
Moon sextile Saturn

A pleasant aspect between the Moon and Saturn will bring progress both in those areas of your life that are open for all to see and also to some kind of secret project of your own.

WEDNESDAY, 19TH MAY
Moon square Jupiter

You may need money to get a project off the ground now and this is a good time to start looking for it. You won't get immediate results from this, but you should keep plugging away until you get the breakthrough that you need. Don't borrow money for unnecessary fripperies but use your credit cards and your borrowing facility wisely.

THURSDAY, 20TH MAY
Moon opposite Neptune

There's very little decision-making going on at the moment. The Lunar opposition to Neptune ensures that either you or your partner will be in a state of confusion unable to make the simplest choices no matter how clearly the issues are expressed. In short, it's a day for dithering. Leave anything complex or vital to another day when minds are more incisive.

FRIDAY, 21ST MAY
Sun into Gemini

The Sun moves into your own sign today bringing with it a lifting of your spirits and a gaining of confidence all round. Your birthday will soon be here and we hope that it will be a good one for you. You may see more of your family than is usual now and there should be some socializing and partying to look forward to. Music belongs to the realm of the Sun, so treat yourself to a musical treat soon.

SATURDAY, 22ND MAY
Uranus retrograde

Uranus turns to retrograde motion today and this will bring some delays and setbacks in various areas of your life over the next few weeks. You may find it difficult to fit in travel plans with other members of the family, or these may clash with your job or with other duties that you have to perform. You may wish to escape from the chores, only to find that you can't. There may be legal or official problems to contend with over the next few weeks too.

GEMINI

SUNDAY, 23RD MAY
Mercury into Gemini

The movement of Mercury into your own sign signals the start of a period of much clearer thinking for you. You will know where you want to go and what you want to do from now on. It will be quite easy for you to influence others with the brilliance of your ideas and you will also be able to project just the right image. Guard against trying to crowd too much into one day today.

MONDAY, 24TH MAY
Moon trine Mercury

This looks like being rather a good day for you, so enjoy yourself. You should be filled with bright ideas today which you are simply raring to put into practice. If, despite all this brilliance, you are still missing a vital piece of information, try asking around among the members of your family or among your neighbours.

TUESDAY, 25TH MAY
Sun trine Neptune

If you talk your problems over with an intelligent and wise friend, this will help you to understand what is going on in your life and possibly bring these troubles to an end. You may be filled with artistic or creative inspiration now which will set you on a course which you may not otherwise have considered. You may find yourself enjoying somebody else's musical or artistic creations today.

WEDNESDAY, 26TH MAY
Sun conjunct Mercury

Mercury and the Sun are in conjunction in your own sign today. This will bring success on many different fronts for you. Mercury is especially effective in regard to any form of communications. Therefore, if you need to get on the phone and to deal with things, you will make excellent progress today. It is a good day for starting projects, finding work or writing of any kind, so get going on that novel you have been thinking of for so long!

THURSDAY, 27TH MAY
Moon square Neptune

You may not be feeling at your best today, either because you are genuinely off-colour, or because you feel uneasy about the atmosphere that is around you at the moment.

GEMINI

FRIDAY, 28TH MAY
Moon square Uranus

It looks as though your normally quick and agile mind will not be working too well today. You may have a head that is stuffed up with catarrh, or your sinuses may be playing you up. You may be perfectly well but just not thinking clearly today. If you have asked a friend to lend you a hand, you will find yourself being let down. Not a great day for anything, unfortunately.

SATURDAY, 29TH MAY
Mars opposite Jupiter

The world is your oyster today – at least, that's how it seems. Though you are pretty exuberant, you mustn't fool yourself into believing that wishful thinking is fact! In affairs of the heart especially, your expectations should not ignore common sense. Try to keep your feet on the ground.

SUNDAY, 30TH MAY
Full Moon

The Full Moon shines in the area of close relationships today. Since it is a stress indicator, you'd be wise to build some bridges within a close partnership now, either that or be content to let an emotional link drift – possibly away! Your understanding and tolerance will be the key to relationship success now.

MONDAY, 31ST MAY
Venus square Mars

They say that a woman's place is in the wrong! Well, today your place is in the wrong, whatever your gender. You won't be able to please anybody, so try pleasing yourself; at least this way somebody will be satisfied! You may find that other people cost you money or that they take up your time on wild-goose chases or in some other way waste your resources. Younger members of the family will be in a touchy mood too.

Claims of over £50,000 must be made in person. **If you believe you have won over £50,000 telephone the National Lottery Line.** For all claims over £500 you will be required to complete a claim form available from a Retailer or by telephoning the National Lottery Line, and show proof of identity. To claim by post, please send your ticket and completed claim form(where required), at your own risk, to The National Lottery, P.O. Box 287, Watford WD18 9TT.

GQ

Name _____

Address _____

_____ Post Code _____

Safe custody of your ticket is your responsibility. If your ticket is lost, stolen, or destroyed, you can make a written claim to Camelot no later than 30 days after the winning draw date, but it will be at Camelot's discretion whether or not to investigate and to pay the claim.

THE OPERATOR OF THE NATIONAL LOTTERY

The National Lottery is run by Camelot Group plc under licence granted by the National Lottery Commission. The principal office of the National Lottery Operator, Camelot Group plc is The National Lottery, Tolpits Lane, Watford WD18 9RN.

GAMES RULES AND PROCEDURES

The game(s) for which this ticket is issued is/are subject to the Rules and Procedures for that game/those games, which set out the contractual rights and obligations of the player and the game(s) promoter (and operator if different). Game(s) Rules and Procedures are available to view at National Lottery On-Line games Retailers, and copies can be obtained from the National Lottery Line. The promoter/operator is entitled to treat this ticket as invalid if the data hereon does not correspond with the entries on Camelot's central computer. Players must be 16 or over.

GQ   Strålfors

THE NATIONAL LOTTERY®

For information about The National Lottery please call the National Lottery Line on 0845 910 0000, or visit our website at www.national-lottery.co.uk. A separate MINICOM line for the hard of hearing is also available. More than 28% of National Lottery proceeds is expected to go to the Good Causes over the period of Camelot's operating licence.

GUIDANCE ON HOW TO PLAY

The name(s) of the game(s) for which this ticket is issued is/are printed overleaf. For how to play and prize structures see the Players' Guide, available from Retailers or the National Lottery Line.

The results can be found through recognised media channels, National Lottery On-Line Retailers or the National Lottery Line.

Tickets issued in error, illegible or incomplete can be cancelled if returned to the issuing terminal within 120 minutes after purchase and before close of ticket sales from that terminal on that day.

GUIDANCE ON HOW TO CLAIM A PRIZE

For details about how and where to claim prizes of various values see the Players' Guide, available at Retailers. If you hold a winning ticket you must claim your prize by post, or in person at a National Lottery Retailer, Post Office or Regional Centre as appropriate, within 180 days of the applicable draw date, or within this period notify the National Lottery Line of your intention to claim, and then claim within 187 days of that draw date.

Claims of over £50,000 must be made in person. **If you believe you have won over £50,000 telephone the National Lottery Line.** For all claims over £500 you will be required to complete a claim form available from a Retailer or by telephoning the National Lottery Line, and show proof of identity. To claim by post, please send your ticket and completed claim form(where required), at your own risk, to The National Lottery, P.O. Box 287, Watford WD18 9TT.

GQ

Name _____

Address _____

_____ Post Code _____

Safe custody of your ticket is your responsibility. If your ticket is lost, stolen, or destroyed, you can make a written claim to Camelot no later than 30 days after the winning draw date, but it will be at Camelot's discretion whether or not to investigate and to pay the claim.

THE OPERATOR OF THE NATIONAL LOTTERY

The National Lottery is run by Camelot Group plc under licence granted by the National Lottery Commission. The principal office of the National Lottery Operator, Camelot Group plc is The National Lottery, Tolpits Lane, Watford WD18 9RN.

Lotto

IT'S A ROLLOVER ON WEDNESDAY
EST £8.5 MILLION JACKPOT
159-10859281-05768

A.	08	11	13	25	28	30
B.	12	15	18	23	25	26
C.	03	06	09	12	21	27
D.	34	36	40	43	45	49
E.	05	09	11	13	14	17
F.	14	31	37	38	40	44
G.	05	07	15	17	26	44

WED09 JUN 04
FOR 01 WED DRAW

013999 RET NO. 102598 £ 7.00
159-10859281-05768
FILL BOX TO VOID

June at a Glance

LOVE	❤	❤	❤	❤	
WORK	★	★	★	★	★
MONEY	£	£	£		
HEALTH	✛	✛	✛		
LUCK	⊍	⊍	⊍	⊍	⊍

TUESDAY, 1ST JUNE
Venus square Jupiter

If a friend asks you for a loan today, think before agreeing. The chances of you getting the money back are probably small but that doesn't mean you shouldn't help your friend. Jon and Sasha suggest that, in these cases, it is better to make an outright gift – maybe of an amount which is smaller than the one asked for – rather than lending money. The laws of karma suggest that any such gift will be returned although probably in a roundabout way and not from the person to whom it was given.

WEDNESDAY, 2ND JUNE
Sun opposite Pluto

There is a great deal of tension around you at the moment and, unfortunately, this situation is not simply going to simmer down and disappear. You are being faced with having to transform some of your relationships with others in some important way. The good news is that the trouble may not affect the relationship between you and your lover but it may well affect some of your other open relationships.

THURSDAY, 3RD JUNE
Mars direct

Mars has occupied your Solar house of leisure, play and romance for some time now, but it has been rolling backwards too. From today, as your ruling planet resumes direct motion, all issues connected with your passions should go better. Any frustrations you've laboured under will fade away giving more satisfaction to your life. In short, fun times are here again!

FRIDAY, 4TH JUNE
Mercury trine Mars

If ever there was a time for romantic words, a forceful expression of personal magnetism and passionate embraces this is it! If you've been shy with the object of your affections, then this is the day to declare your love openly.

SATURDAY, 5TH JUNE
Venus into Leo

If you've got any favours to ask, the passage of Venus into your Solar house of persuasion shows that you can use considerable charm and eloquence to win others over to your point of view with little trouble at all. A little flirtation combined with a winning way ensures that you achieve your desires. Your creative talents are boosted too so perhaps you should consider writing down your inspirations now.

SUNDAY, 6TH JUNE
Moon square Pluto

You will have some difficulty in relating to others today. There may be a conflict of interest between the demands of your job and those of your partner or of close friends. For example, you may have to cancel an arrangement with a friend or a lover because of work. On the other hand, you may oblige your pals, only to get behind in your work and find that the boss is on your tail as a result.

MONDAY, 7TH JUNE
Mercury into Cancer

All the planets seem to be restless just now since Mercury changes sign today. At least you can get your mind into gear concerning the state of your finances now. Tasks you've been putting off like cancelling useless standing orders, or ensuring you receive the most advantageous interest from your savings will be tackled with ease now.

TUESDAY, 8TH JUNE
Sun trine Uranus

You are in an exuberant and quite outrageous mood today. Since you'll be game for a laugh you'll be prepared to shock others out of complacency by pointing out certain flaws in their arguments and highlighting their prejudices. Though this will be done for the best possible reasons, you'll enjoy rupturing their pomposity too!

GEMINI

WEDNESDAY, 9TH JUNE
Moon sextile Uranus

If you have been trying to put things right between you and your friends or if you have been putting up with some kind of unpleasantness from one, so-called friend, then the events of today will help to put things right. Another person, perhaps outside your actual circle, may be just the right person to help you deal with this. Your philosophy of life is changing now and you will come out of this thinking differently.

THURSDAY, 10TH JUNE
Venus opposite Neptune

If female friends pass on gossip, information or even hard news of some kind today, do be careful to check their sources and to make sure that what they are telling you is the truth. Your friends and colleagues are not out to deceive you deliberately (we hope?) but they may be unwittingly passing on duff information to you and to others. You may have some kind of vaguely spooky experience which unnerves you too today.

FRIDAY, 11TH JUNE
Moon square Uranus

Something rather nasty will come out of the woodwork at you today and the chances are that a woman will be at the back of it. You may be the subject of gossip or you may simply be on the receiving end of someone else's spiteful tongue. Your beliefs may be questioned and you could even find yourself accused of having the wrong values or of being prejudiced.

SATURDAY, 12TH JUNE
Moon trine Neptune

Something will happen which puts your mind at rest now. None of this will be straightforward because the news which you hear or the relief which you feel will come from an unusual or unexpected source. You will now feel free to pursue your own interests and to follow your heart in some matter. Romance could come to some of you but this too would come from a peculiar or unexpected place or through an unusual person in some way.

SUNDAY, 13TH JUNE
New Moon

There's a New Moon in your own sign. This is a powerfully positive influence that encourages you to make a new start. Personal opportunities are about to change your life. You must now be prepared to leave the past behind to embark on a brand new course. Decide what you want, because you'll be your own best guide now.

MONDAY, 14TH JUNE
Venus trine Pluto

If you were thinking of popping the question, or indeed waiting for the question to be popped, this could be the day. The romance of Venus unites with the sultry passion of Pluto showing that intimate affairs are about to be spoken of.

TUESDAY, 15TH JUNE
Mercury sextile Saturn

Financial obstacles that have faced you are starting to look as though they won't be a problem for long. Some words of advice from a trustworthy person will put your monetary position in a far more positive light. A realistic, but not depressive attitude will work wonders for both your confidence and your cash flow.

WEDNESDAY, 16TH JUNE
Sun trine Mars

You're a regular dynamo today! The powerful positive influences of the Sun and Mars give you enormous energy and enthusiasm. You're in the mood for fun and will throw yourself heart and soul into any activity that takes your fancy. Artistic talent, romance and any and all creative potentials should flourish.

THURSDAY, 17TH JUNE
Moon opposite Uranus

There will be a great deal of surprising news today, some of which could come your way via sisters, brothers or neighbours. You may also have to make a sudden adjustment to your travel plans. The answer to all this is to take a flexible attitude to everything and to be prepared to make changes while on the run. If you try to 'mother' someone close to you, they will resist this and accuse you of smothering them instead.

FRIDAY, 18TH JUNE
Moon trine Jupiter

You will have chatted to so many people by the end of today that your voice will probably be hoarse. All your friends will phone you up, neighbours will stop you in the street, relatives whom you don't talk to from one year's end to another will come round to see you and gossip will flow in and out from all quarters. There will be great news in the post and even your local paper will have something special in it just for you.

GEMINI

SATURDAY, 19TH JUNE
Venus square Saturn

A host of minor worries are revealed by today's square aspect between Venus and Saturn. It's important not to over-react when you feel that communication with a lover is too cool for comfort. Before you jump to any conclusions you should play the waiting game and see what this evening brings.

SUNDAY, 20TH JUNE
Sun sextile Jupiter

This is a good day in which to take a small gamble. Don't take this too seriously but a small wager should come up trumps. There may be a windfall of some other kind and another possibility is that a friend may share a piece of good luck or good news with you by taking you out for a drink or a meal. You may book up a trip on an impulse now or you may decide to get involved in something 'New Agey' like astrology or the Tarot.

MONDAY, 21ST JUNE
Sun into Cancer

Your financial prospects take an upturn from today as the Sun enters your house of money and possessions. The next month should see an improvement in your economic security. It may be that you need to lay plans to ensure maximum profit now. Don't expect any swift returns for investments but lay down a pattern for future growth. Sensible monetary decisions made now will pay off in a big way.

TUESDAY, 22ND JUNE
Venus opposite Uranus

Feelings run high today and harsh words are likely to be spoken. An unexpected reaction to an idle comment will lead you to the conclusion that the emotional undercurrents run very deep indeed. Tread carefully!

WEDNESDAY, 23RD JUNE
Mercury square Mars

There could be considerable tension between you and the younger members of the family now. They may be going that bit too far and taking your good nature for granted or being thoughtless or careless in some way. Ask yourself if what you want them is reasonable and, if the answer is yes, then insist on it. You may find that your lover doesn't share your priorities today and this could also cause a bit of tension.

THURSDAY, 24TH JUNE
Moon opposite Saturn

You really mustn't expect everything to go just the way you want every day. The optimism could be seriously knocked now as the Moon opposes the sober planet Saturn. You'll be made very aware of all those circumstances that restrict your progress, and if you don't take care, you'll be plunged in a pit of gloom. Try to take a realistic look at the way things are going without giving in to depression and you'll arrive at a reasonable assessment of where you actually are. It's better than it looks.

FRIDAY, 25TH JUNE
Mercury square Jupiter

Your intentions may be good but you must also have your head screwed on the right way round. Therefore, if you intend to get involved with any kind of business venture or money matter with friends, then make sure that this is on a totally professional footing right from the start. Working partnerships should also be kept on a strictly business footing for the time being.

SATURDAY, 26TH JUNE
Mercury into Leo

Your mind will be going at full speed ahead over the next few weeks and you are bound to come up with some really great new ideas. You will be very busy with the phone ringing off its hook and letters falling into your letter box by the ton. You will find yourself acting as a temporary secretary for a while, even if the only person who makes use of your services is yourself.

SUNDAY, 27TH JUNE
Moon trine Venus

Any problems that have been plaguing your personal relationships will melt away today. They may return at another time but for now peace and quiet will reign. A female friend will do much to calm you down and to help you to regain your sense of humour and also to regain your sense of proportion.

MONDAY, 28TH JUNE
Jupiter into Taurus

Your capacity for sympathy and compassion is greatly enhanced by the movement of Jupiter into the most private area of your chart from today. You will be ready, even eager to help others through troubles with no thought of personal gain. Take care that you are not led astray by glib liars.

TUESDAY, 29TH JUNE
Moon trine Saturn

You won't be in the most social of moods today. Perhaps there's some serious financial matter that needs your undivided attention. You won't be happy until it's out of the way so seclude yourself and get on with it.

WEDNESDAY, 30TH JUNE
Mercury opposite Neptune

This is not going to be a great day for travelling or for clear communication. Mercury, the planet of clear thought and movement, is enmeshed in the confusing influence of Neptune so it would be best to stick close to home and not involve yourself in any controversies.

July at a Glance

LOVE	❤	❤			
WORK	★	★	★	★	★
MONEY	£				
HEALTH	✪	✪	✪	✪	
LUCK	U	U	U	U	

THURSDAY, 1ST JULY
Moon sextile Pluto

Your emotional condition depends on the behaviour of those who are around you today. Therefore, if your lover and your family are happy and co-operative, you will be happy too, but if they are tense and restless, this will affect your mood. You could do well to sort out any joint legal or official matters now because these things will go smoothly and also more quickly than they normally do.

FRIDAY, 2ND JULY
Moon opposite Venus

You aren't on top form emotionally today. In fact, your vulnerability is such that you couldn't put up any resistance to pressure or emotional blackmail now. You'd far rather follow the crowd than stand out in any way. You're very anxious to please, but this is a trait that shouldn't be taken too far. Serious decisions about the state of your relationship will have to be put off until you are feeling stronger.

SATURDAY, 3RD JULY
Moon trine Mars

If there has been some kind of financial or business delay recently, this should soon pass and you will be able to get on faster than you could before. A youngish man may be extremely helpful where quite serious matters are concerned. You may, for instance, consult a youngish man in a professional capacity, either as a doctor, a lawyer or some other kind of professional adviser.

SUNDAY, 4TH JULY
Mars opposite Jupiter

Don't allow yourself to lose your temper in the workplace today. You may feel let down, or that a doorway has been closed to you. If that's so, then there's a good reason and you may have escaped a difficult and thankless task. Keep looking around, your luck will change very soon.

MONDAY, 5TH JULY
Mars into Scorpio

Mars enters your Solar sixth house of work and duties to others. This house also rules health matters. This planetary movement will help to bring the blockages of the last few weeks to an end, allowing you to settle into a much more suitable working routine over the next few months. This invigorating planet should bring a boost to your immune system, so if you have been ill lately, recovery is on the way. Watch your teeth however, and be prepared for a visit to the dentist.

TUESDAY, 6TH JULY
Moon square Sun

You may decide to treat a friend to a meal out or to a small luxury of some kind. This would be a great idea if you could be sure that your friend would appreciate your generosity. Unfortunately, he or she may take this for granted and your efforts will be wasted.

WEDNESDAY, 7TH JULY
Moon trine Venus

A chat with a woman friend may be just the thing to help you get things into perspective today. You seem to need some kind of practical advice in order to prevent you from taking a rather foolish course of action. A pal may suggest an unexpected and rather unusual outing later in the day and you would be missing a lot of fun if you turn this down.

THURSDAY, 8TH JULY
Mercury trine Pluto

Relationship problems should be solved easily today since you are extra perceptive and able to approach the most delicate subject with tact and diplomacy. You can reassure your partner and soothe fears with a few well-chosen words now.

FRIDAY, 9TH JULY
Moon square Venus

There are some days when you just want to be left alone with your own thoughts. Unfortunately, your popularity is such that others are anxious for your company. If you really want solitude, then you'll have to pretend that you're out. Don't answer the door or the phone. Relax, surround yourself with music and sink back into your favourite chair. Alternatively, a long walk in the fresh air will restore your spirits.

SATURDAY, 10TH JULY
Moon sextile Mercury

Being too proud to talk over a problem is a self-defeating attitude. A relative may find himself or herself in just such a situation and need encouragement. All you have to do is listen because the problem could well be solved by simply talking about it. Just smile and nod in the appropriate places and you'll both be OK.

SUNDAY, 11TH JULY
Mars square Neptune

The triviality of everyday life and the pettiness of work-mates will really get you down today. You need novelty and a break from the mundane. There'll be no point in taking your frustrations out on others because they simply won't understand. At least your dreams are your own.

MONDAY, 12TH JULY
Mercury retrograde

Whenever Mercury moves into retrograde motion, you can expect a short period of muddle and misunderstandings. This is not a good time in which to try to sort out arguments or differences in business if you can avoid it. Leave everyone to simmer down for a while and if the situation still needs a few words in two or three weeks' time, have a go at it then.

GEMINI

TUESDAY, 13TH JULY
New Moon

Today's New Moon shows that your financial affairs have reached a point where you have to make a decision. Do you carry on in the old, and rather dreary ways of making and spending your cash or will you look at the realities and make sensible decisions? This isn't a time to retreat into dreamland, or to carry on with bad budgeting. Look at your monetary state carefully now.

WEDNESDAY, 14TH JULY
Moon conjunct Mercury

You might think that you speak in a reasoned, clear voice today but your emotional intensity is showing through. You've obviously got a lot of conviction now and you can't fail to be persuasive and eloquent when you display such sincerity. If a close partnership has been going through a sticky patch, then it's time you expressed your true feelings.

THURSDAY, 15TH JULY
Venus trine Jupiter

There's nothing more important to you than harmony in your home at the moment. You need a breather, away from the trials of your working life. The more stable your family makes you feel now, the better for your psychological health. A fulsome expression of affection towards you will make you feel worthwhile.

FRIDAY, 16TH JULY
Mercury trine Pluto

A conversation with a loved one will get very intense later on. You may find out things about a partner that you hadn't even suspected! The good news is that this information is more likely to relieve your worries rather than cause any!

SATURDAY, 17TH JULY
Void Moon

The Moon is 'void of course' today, so don't bother with anything important and don't start anything new now. Stick to your usual routines and don't change your lifestyle in any way.

SUNDAY, 18TH JULY
Saturn square Uranus

There's a celestial tug-of-war going on between Saturn and Uranus today, with you as the rope! An urge to break out of the dreary and mundane is combated by a more prosaic and common-sense view provided by the ringed planet. I wonder which one will win.

MONDAY, 19TH JULY
Moon trine Uranus

You seem to be filled with some kind of magical charisma today which will attract the opposite sex like bees to a honey-pot! You may fall head over heels in love with a devastatingly attractive person, or you may find that someone else has fallen crazily in love with you. Your sense of proportion and perspective will go completely off-centre and you won't know whether you are coming or going now.

TUESDAY, 20TH JULY
Moon square Sun

The quest for happiness can sometimes be more expensive than you expect. All you want to do is have some fun, but how far are you prepared to go to find it? It could be that you are trying to escape from an unpleasant fact of life by drowning your sorrows.

WEDNESDAY, 21ST JULY
Jupiter square Neptune

Reality scarce gets a look in when Jupiter and Neptune befuddle your mind with dreams of far-off places and an exotic lifestyle that is way out of range of your pocket. Dreams are fine, but when they replace real life then beware!

THURSDAY, 22ND JULY
Mercury square Mars

Being a person with a fiery nature it's sometimes too easy to express the full force of your personality without realizing how aggressive you actually seem. Verbal aggression is the problem today and you could offend the sensibilities of someone you wouldn't hurt for the world. If in doubt, hold your tongue.

FRIDAY, 23RD JULY
Sun into Leo

Your curiosity will be massively stimulated from today as the Sun enters the area of learning and communication. Other people's business suddenly becomes your own now. That's not to say that you turn into a busybody overnight, it's just that many will turn to you for some guidance. Affairs in the lives of your brothers, sisters and neighbours have extra importance now. Short journeys too are well starred for one month.

GEMINI

SATURDAY, 24TH JULY
Moon sextile Uranus

Today has the feeling of a breakthrough time about it. You will be able to find unusual and original ways of solving problems and, even if your mind is not at its best, your friends will come to your rescue with some great ideas of their own. You may decide to take a trip now or to look through your brochures (and your options) in order to plan one for the future. You are happy but a bit restless.

SUNDAY, 25TH JULY
Mercury square Jupiter

Wishful thinking isn't usually a fault to one of your down-to-earth nature, but today the mixed influence of Mercury and Jupiter don't encourage you to take the practical view. In most areas you're idealistic and dreamy. No matter what boring duties you're involved with, your mind is definitely in a world of its own.

MONDAY, 26TH JULY
Sun opposite Neptune

The Sun opposes confusing Neptune today so nothing will go to plan. Major tasks should be avoided and gossip completely ignored. This is a time of misunderstandings, so take care.

TUESDAY, 27TH JULY
Sun square Jupiter

It's a day to put some effort into being understanding today. The Sun is in harsh aspect to Jupiter, an aspect which tends to increase your capacity for natural cynicism. You'll be prepared to think the worst of anything or anyone at the moment but you could be surprised. If you're involved in any sort of conflict, try to see the other person's point of view. It'll save you a lot of grief in the long run.

WEDNESDAY, 28TH JULY
Full Moon eclipse

Eclipses often show endings but that's not necessarily a bad thing. If you've been involved with college courses or any kind of educational matter, this eclipse could show a successful conclusion to your efforts. Problems in the lives of brothers or sisters could also cease at this time.

THURSDAY, 29TH JULY
Moon square Saturn

Delays and frustrations abound on a day when the Moon makes a stressful aspect to Saturn. Anything connected with learning or travel is most prone to distraction and petty annoyances. Keep calm, today may be challenging but you'll win through.

FRIDAY, 30TH JULY
Sun trine Pluto

In all partnership affairs you will be in the dominant position today. Your other half and business associates will look to you for leadership and guidance. Something that you can and will provide. You must admit it's been needed for a while!

SATURDAY, 31ST JULY
Mercury into Cancer retrograde

Mercury re-enters your Solar area of finances today, which is not a good indication of prosperity. Take care of the cash and don't go in for any HP deals now.

August at a Glance

LOVE	❤	❤	❤		
WORK	★	★	★	★	
MONEY	£	£	£		
HEALTH	✪	✪	✪	✪	
LUCK	☒	☒	☒	☒	☒

SUNDAY, 1ST AUGUST
Moon trine Mercury

It's important to keep your ears open now, for a hint will be dropped that could do your career prospects some good. In work affairs you may have been prone to anxiety about your job security, but the news you hear today should put your mind at rest. In all dealings with authority, if you want anything done go straight to the top.

MONDAY, 2ND AUGUST
Moon trine Sun

You and your family will enjoy quite a bit of company around the house now. If you decide to do some entertaining, you will find it exciting and very successful if you mix up the age groups and if you bring people of different backgrounds and ideas together. People will be happy to hear what you have to say and you will be just as fascinated to listen to their pearls of wisdom.

TUESDAY, 3RD AUGUST
Venus trine Jupiter

An exuberant mood is evident today giving you the confidence to express yourself in your surroundings. You may wish to create a personal pleasure palace in your own home, and you can be sure that you have the excellent taste and vision to do just that!

WEDNESDAY, 4TH AUGUST
Moon trine Venus

The finer things of life have a delightful appeal today. You're in a cultured frame of mind susceptible to refined music and fine art. There's also a romantic side to this Venusian influence, so it's a time to indulge yourself in pleasure.

THURSDAY, 5TH AUGUST
Moon conjunct Saturn

It's obviously a day for deep thinking when the Moon conjuncts Saturn in your Solar house of psychology. There's no guessing what's going on in your mind now. The only danger here is that you tend to dwell on the more negative aspects of your life while ignoring the happy things. If you find yourself blowing your problems out of proportion seek out a friend for a chat. A problem shared is a problem halved.

FRIDAY, 6TH AUGUST
Mercury direct

The wayward planet Mercury resumes a direct motion today which will restore some order from the chaos that has beset your economic interests. Don't expect instant miracles though. The mass of paperwork and financial complication that has piled up while your attention was diverted will take some sorting out. At least now you're in a positive frame of mind and capable of handling the most vexed monetary questions with relative ease.

SATURDAY, 7TH AUGUST
Sun square Mars

More haste, less speed! In work affairs especially, your own impatience and irritable attitudes could easily alienate colleagues and friends who do want to help. What you need is a plan. A few moments thinking through your means and intentions before you start will save enormous hassle later.

GEMINI

SUNDAY, 8TH AUGUST
Sun opposite Uranus

Unusual and unexpected news will have you scuttling hither and thither at a moment's notice. You may decide to take a sudden trip abroad or to do something drastic about changing your usual mode of transport. Something that a friend says to you could have the effect of making you change your usual way of looking at life and of beginning to assess yourself and your surrounding world in a very different way.

MONDAY, 9TH AUGUST
Moon sextile Saturn

Though Lunar aspects to Saturn often indicate hard work, today's events will show that all your efforts are about to pay off. Money should come in, not by luck, but because you've worked hard for it.

TUESDAY, 10TH AUGUST
Sun square Saturn

Though you are clear about your own mind and what you want to accomplish, you can't seem to explain your position or make any progress today. Talking at cross-purposes, unexplained prejudice and downright stubbornness are a few of the obstacles you'll meet with now. Try to be patient, and hold to your common sense because that's the only thing you can rely on now.

WEDNESDAY, 11TH AUGUST
New Moon eclipse

According to Nostradamus today is 'Doomsday'! However, Sasha and Jonathan aren't as pessimistic as he was even if there is an eclipse! Eclipses were feared by ancient astrologers. However, these events take place about four times a year, so they are not unusual. Their effects can be mildly irritating or even, on occasion, absolutely devastating, depending upon whether they fall upon a sensitive point in one's own horoscope. Even when the worse comes to the worst, you end up knowing exactly what the score is, and perhaps that is no bad thing after all.

THURSDAY, 12TH AUGUST
Mercury into Leo

Your life is going to be extremely busy for a while now and there will be little time to sit around and rest. You will have more to do with friends, relatives, colleagues and neighbours than is usual and you could spend quite a bit of time sorting out minor domestic and work problems with workmen and women of various kinds. You may also spend time and money sorting out a vehicle.

GEMINI

FRIDAY, 13TH AUGUST
Mercury opposite Neptune

Don't be led astray by way-out ideas no matter how attractive they seem. You are more than slightly gullible at the moment so you could be taken in by anything! Try not to travel far either, since stupid incidents will spoil your fun.

SATURDAY, 14TH AUGUST
Mars opposite Saturn

Bad feeling in the workplace could have a damaging effect on your morale if you involve yourself in plots and silly schemes. Keep your head down and attend to your own affairs if you want an easy life.

SUNDAY, 15TH AUGUST
Venus into Leo retrograde

Some days you just can't say anything right! This is one I'm afraid because Venus adds an element of emotional confusion to all your verbal expression. Don't try to write letters full of meaning because you're likely to give the wrong impression.

MONDAY, 16TH AUGUST
Moon sextile Sun

It's a day for simple pleasures and innocent enjoyment. A quiet conversation with a child or younger person should show you that you can still learn a thing or two, and have a laugh as well.

TUESDAY, 17TH AUGUST
Mercury squares Jupiter

Wishful thinking isn't usually a fault of one of your down-to-earth nature, but today the mixed influence of Mercury and Jupiter don't encourage you to take the practical view. In most areas you're idealistic and dreamy. No matter what boring duties you're involved with, your mind is definitely in a world of its own.

WEDNESDAY, 18TH AUGUST
Moon opposite Saturn

You may feel a little under the weather today. The Moon's opposition to Saturn casts an aura of gloom over you. It's probably work pressure that's at the root of your mood and you desperately need some light relief. Keep away from arduous tasks now. Be easy on yourself or your health may suffer.

GEMINI

THURSDAY, 19TH AUGUST
Pluto direct

Any partnership matters which have been held up in the works will get moving very quickly now. This means, depending upon your personal circumstances, that you could get contracts or joint ventures off the ground now or that you and a lover could move towards a happy future with more confidence from now on. You may find yourself dealing with legal or professional people now, but the outcome of this would be good.

FRIDAY, 20TH AUGUST
Sun conjunct Venus

What a great day to fall in love! Even if you are in a rock-solid relationship, you could discover more about your partner than you knew before and this discovery will only make you love him or her all the more. This is the time to take a chance on life and love and to tell the object of your affections just how deep your feelings really are.

SATURDAY, 21ST AUGUST
Moon trines Venus

There's a happy aura of peace and romance about today's stars. The Moon combines with Venus bringing you into perfect harmony with your partner in life. If you are unattached, then a casual conversation will reveal that you've got a lot in common with a new friend. This relationship could deepen into something far more meaningful.

SUNDAY, 22ND AUGUST
Moon trine Jupiter

This should be a very optimistic and forward-looking day. Any pressures on you will seem lighter and you'll be sure that you can handle anything the world cares to throw at you. When it comes to financial planning, there are few who could match you in shrewdness. You may even feel inclined to celebrate this time of light relief by treating yourself to an outing.

MONDAY, 23RD AUGUST
Sun into Virgo

The home and family become your main interest over the next four weeks as the Sun moves into the most domestic area of your chart from today. Family feuds will now be resolved, and you'll find an increasing contentment in your own surroundings. A haven of peace will be restored in your home. This should also be a period of nostalgia when happy memories come flooding back.

TUESDAY, 24TH AUGUST
Venus square Mars

The demands of your working world will be heavy today, and you may feel the effects of stress. Possibly in the form of headaches of backache. The harsh aspect between Venus and Mars shows how far you've got to got to make your ideas a reality. This is not a signal to be downhearted however. Look after your own well-being today and you'll soon be back in fighting form.

WEDNESDAY, 25TH AUGUST
Jupiter retrograde

Jupiter, the planet of luck, comes to a halt today, so you may feel that your good fortune has deserted you – which is not the case. However, this could be an opportunity to reassess your aims, to forget wishful thinking and to base your ambitions on the firm bedrock of reality.

THURSDAY, 26TH AUGUST
Full Moon

Today's Full Moon shows that important decisions have to be made at a time of rapidly changing circumstances. News that arrives today could well be disturbing yet will prove to be a blessing in disguise in the long run. You may be considering a move of home, possibly to a distant location, or even throwing in your present career to take up an educational course of some kind. People you meet while travelling will have important words to say.

FRIDAY, 27TH AUGUST
Mercury conjunct Venus

Communication will be the name of the game today, so get on the phone, write all those letters and be ready to run errands for yourself and for others. You need to sort out your diary now and to clear the decks for the future because you seem destined to be running into a period of hard work as well as a packed social life. Any feelings of fatigue and malaise will slip away now and you will be energetic once again.

SATURDAY, 28TH AUGUST
Sun trine Jupiter

This is an excellent day. How could it fail to be when the Sun and Jupiter enter a marvellous aspect which puts you on top of the world? Your mood will be light and positive even if there's nothing obvious to be exuberant about. Many will hear news of a celebration in the family, while others will experience a contentment that is spiritual in nature.

SUNDAY, 29TH AUGUST
Moon trine Pluto

Relationships of all kinds will go very smoothly today and you may decide that this is the time to make something which was fairly casual into a much deeper kind of matter. Friends could be instrumental in helping you to sort out some part of your life which has become muddled and this could result in your having a much clearer idea of what you want from others. You may transform a relationship in some way.

MONDAY, 30TH AUGUST
Saturn retrograde

The distant planet Saturn goes into retrograde motion from today indicating a period when you will look within yourself. Introspection and a deep sense of compassion are shown for the next couple of months.

TUESDAY, 31ST AUGUST
Mercury into Virgo

The past exerts a powerful influence as Mercury enters the house of heritage. You'll find that things long forgotten will somehow re-enter your life over the next couple of weeks. An interest in your family heritage may develop, or possibly a new-found passion for antiques. Some good, meaningful conversations in the family will prove enlightening.

September at a Glance

LOVE	❤	❤	❤	❤
WORK	★			
MONEY	£	£	£	
HEALTH	✚	✚	✚	
LUCK	☹			

WEDNESDAY, 1ST SEPTEMBER
Moon square Venus

This is a tense and touchy day. You may trip over your tongue and unintentionally insult some sensitive soul or you may feel upset and unsettled yourself over someone else's insensitive remarks. This is no big deal and it wouldn't be worth falling out over but you may well end up feeling rather miffed. You may also be looking and feeling slightly under the weather now.

THURSDAY, 2ND SEPTEMBER
Mars into Sagittarius

Today, Mars moves into the area of your chart that is devoted to relationships. This planetary situation is like a double-edged sword because, on the one hand, it could bring you closer with your partner or loved one while, on the other hand, it can cause you to become extremely angry at the behaviour of others.

FRIDAY, 3RD SEPTEMBER
Mercury trine Jupiter

Your sense of humour is pretty obvious today when the good-natured planets Mercury and Jupiter team up to show you the funny and bizarre side to the most serious situations. You can't help laughing at the pretensions of those around you. Relatives particularly are shown up in their true colours, a situation too hilarious not to share. Having said that, there's nothing cruel in this display of humour. Just a sense of irony and mild satire.

SATURDAY, 4TH SEPTEMBER
Mercury square Pluto

This will be an awkward day in which other people let you down and leave you to sort out the wreckage. You are in the mood to talk but you partner seems to be afflicted by temporary deafness and an inability to see things from your point of view. You should avoid signing anything binding today, possibly because you haven't looked at all the implications of what you are agreeing to.

SUNDAY, 5TH SEPTEMBER
Moon sextile Saturn

You've got money on your mind today! The Moon and Saturn team up to come up with a sensible solution to debt and related problems. Today's forecast may not be glamorous, but it will set you up for the future.

MONDAY, 6TH SEPTEMBER
Mars sextile Neptune

If you are at all sporty then this is the day for you. Anything energetic will be a lot of fun especially if you are part of a team. It doesn't have to be serious or even very competitive as long as you enjoy yourself.

GEMINI

TUESDAY, 7TH SEPTEMBER
Moon opposite Uranus

You may find yourself taking a sudden and unexpected journey which keeps you away from home for a while. This may be a spur-of-the-moment visit to friends or family or it could be something much more exciting. Another strong possibility is that a journey which you have already planned right down to the last detail, could suddenly go completely haywire. One thing for sure is that you won't finish the day where you expected to be!

WEDNESDAY, 8TH SEPTEMBER
Sun conjunct Mercury

A good chat with a relative could open up possibilities and reveal old secrets today. The Sun meets up with Mercury in your Solar house of heritage and family issues so you'll take a great deal of pleasure in the company of those who are close to you. This should also be a time to look to the future. Perhaps a move of home should be considered now.

THURSDAY, 9TH SEPTEMBER
New Moon

The New Moon falls in the sphere of home and family today indicating a need for a change. For some reason you've been dissatisfied with your domestic set-up so you may consider looking at house prices in your own, or indeed another area. You probably feel that you need more space and light in your life that your present home isn't providing. A family member may be considering setting up home independently and deserves all the encouragement you can give.

FRIDAY, 10TH SEPTEMBER
Sun trine Saturn

The Sun's aspect to Saturn puts everything in perspective today. In fact, you'll be anxious to put every area of your life in order now. The home is the main scene of your reforming zeal. 'A place for everything, and everything in its place' is your motto for this practical day.

SATURDAY, 11TH SEPTEMBER
Venus direct

Venus returns to direct motion and brings an ease of communication and a charm in your verbal expression with it. If you've had any problems with neighbours or your own family, you can now smooth these over with your exceptional charm.

GEMINI

SUNDAY, 12TH SEPTEMBER
Moon sextile Venus

A long chat to a woman friend is just what you need to get your life into perspective. Talking over old times, or indeed times to come, a gossip and a laugh or two will set you up for anything the world could possibly throw at you.

MONDAY, 13TH SEPTEMBER
Moon square Neptune

You might not know what it is exactly that you want to do today, but you'll know that it isn't what you are doing. You could be feeling pretty restless, but until somebody comes up with a workable suggestion, you'll be in the dark I'm afraid.

TUESDAY, 14TH SEPTEMBER
Moon opposite Saturn

You may feel out of sorts today. A niggling ailment will be extremely irritating. Aching knees or other joints could be the symptom that troubles you most. On the other hand, the teeth could be playing up or just extra sensitive.

WEDNESDAY, 15TH SEPTEMBER
Mars conjunct Pluto

You may come to an important decision today regarding a person who matters greatly to you. You may decide to live with or even to marry a particular partner. You may begin a business partnership or you may bring one to an end. It is really rather unlikely that you would break up an important relationship of any kind today, because the stars suggest beginnings rather than endings just now.

THURSDAY, 16TH SEPTEMBER
Mercury into Libra

Mercury moves into a part of your horoscope that is concerned with creativity. Mercury rules such things as thinking, learning and communications, but it can also be associated with skills and craftwork of various kinds. The combination of creativity and craftwork suggest that the next few weeks would be a good time to work on hobbies such as dressmaking, carpentry and so on.

FRIDAY, 17TH SEPTEMBER
Mercury trine Neptune

You will be on the receiving end of a great deal of help today and this may come from some rather odd sources. A neighbour may come up with an out-of-the-blue offer to help look after an animal or even a child for a while. A younger member of the family may astonish you by putting him or herself out on your behalf. You may even be aware of something strange, such as spiritual help from the 'other side'.

SATURDAY, 18TH SEPTEMBER
Moon square Mercury

This is not the day to take any chances, especially where love or money is concerned. This is a great day, however, to visit a theatre, comedy store or a nightclub because you will be joyfully entertained by a witty and funny comedian or comedienne. Be careful while operating communications machinery or while driving today.

SUNDAY, 19TH SEPTEMBER
Moon trine Saturn

You'll do best if you are self-reliant today. You could spot a detail that will enable you to make some money, but you'll only do this if you are left to your own devices in peace.

MONDAY, 20TH SEPTEMBER
Moon trine Sun

Today brings a much needed boost to your confidence and a really welcome smile to your lips. You will feel content within yourself and you will be a hot favourite among others. Your outer manner and your inner feelings are comfortable with each other and you are not at odds with yourself or with anyone else.

TUESDAY, 21ST SEPTEMBER
Mercury sextile Pluto

Every relationship has certain no-go areas where each partner has to tread with care. However today, Mercury's aspect to Pluto opens up some of these unresolved issues and makes talking about them relatively easy. A renewed understanding is possible now.

WEDNESDAY, 22ND SEPTEMBER
Moon opposite Venus

Travel plans may have to be put on the back burner for the time being, possibly due to some kind of family crisis. Female members of the family may not be able to go where you want them to, or they may not be able to get the time off to go when you want them to. Delays and setbacks to all kinds of journeys seem inevitable and travelling at this time could also prove to be more expensive than you had budgeted for.

THURSDAY, 23RD SEPTEMBER
Sun into Libra

You are going to be in a slightly frivolous frame of mind over the next few weeks and you shouldn't punish yourself for this. Pay attention to a creative interest or a demanding hobby now or get involved in something creative on behalf of others. A couple of typical examples would be the production of a school play or making preparations for a flower and vegetable show.

FRIDAY, 24TH SEPTEMBER
Mars sextile Uranus

Wild romance is in the stars today! Mars and Uranus demand an expression of your passionate inner self. A meeting in an odd place may lead to love. It may not last long, but it'll be fun finding out if this new attraction has got staying power!

SATURDAY, 25TH SEPTEMBER
Full Moon

Today's Full Moon could make you feel a bit tetchy and tense and it could also bring you some sort of unexpected expense. The best thing to do today is to stick to your usual routine and not start anything new or important. Jog along as usual and try not to become caught up in anybody else's bad mood now.

SUNDAY, 26TH SEPTEMBER
Moon opposite Mercury

You may hear some disappointing news today, possibly in connection with a friend or with children and youngsters. You may have to cancel plans connected to these people, either because they can't join you today or because you are too busy elsewhere to be bothered with them.

MONDAY, 27TH SEPTEMBER
Moon square Neptune

You are in a solitary mood today, needing to be left alone with your own thoughts. Extremely sensitive, the slightest upset could wound you deeply so it wouldn't be wise to involve yourself with brash or tactless people. It would do you good to remember that, although you are feeling vulnerable, this may not be apparent to others.

TUESDAY, 28TH SEPTEMBER
Moon conjunct Saturn

Independence has got a down side too. It's never been more apparent than today, when all that pioneering energy merely leaves you feeling isolated and out in the cold. You feel as if no one truly understands what you're about. Perhaps they don't but give them time and they'll eventually catch up with your ideas.

WEDNESDAY, 29TH SEPTEMBER
Moon trine Neptune

There is a wonderfully romantic feeling to the day today and this could lead to a pleasant flirtation or two with the most unlikely of people. You may hear good news from family members who are at a distance to you now and this may include an invitation to go and visit them at some time. If you have any legal worries, there could be a rather strange and mysterious event which makes them melt away now.

THURSDAY, 30TH SEPTEMBER
Moon trine Uranus

You are in an excellent mood today. Your personality shines, and your originality is obvious for all to see. You may, however, feel rather restless and dissatisfied with the normal run of things, but that's only to be expected from such a supreme individualist.

October at a Glance

LOVE	❤				
WORK	★	★	★		
MONEY	£				
HEALTH	✪	✪	✪	✪	✪
LUCK	♘	♘	♘	♘	

FRIDAY, 1ST OCTOBER
Sun sextile Pluto

The aspect between the Sun and Pluto could transform your personal life. Those who are married or otherwise linked will find their relationships entering a new phase. If you are single you could find the love of your life.

SATURDAY, 2ND OCTOBER
Mercury sextile Venus

You may think that you know the answer to everything but today you will realize that you have a lot to learn. You may, therefore, decide to take a course of some kind or to improve a particular skill. This may be something practical and useful, such as bricklaying or car-maintenance but it could just as well be something just for fun, such as learning to play an instrument.

SUNDAY, 3RD OCTOBER
Moon square Mercury

You may not feel much like it but today, you need to look into your financial situation and work out a sensible budget for the future. So get out those bank statements and look at your credit card statements and be honest with yourself before you find yourself right off the financial rails. You may feel like going out and enjoying yourself today but duty calls and, therefore, it doesn't look as if you will achieve this.

MONDAY, 4TH OCTOBER
Moon sextile Sun

A woman may have some surprising news for you today and, fortunately, it looks as if the news is likely to be good. Children may surprise you in a particularly pleasant way today too.

TUESDAY, 5TH OCTOBER
Mercury into Scorpio

The movement of Mercury into your Solar sixth house of work, duties and health suggests that a slightly more serious phase is on the way. Over the next three weeks or so you will have to concentrate on what needs to be done rather than on having a good time. You may have a fair bit to do with neighbours, colleagues and relatives of around your own age group soon and you will have to spend a fair bit of time on the phone to them.

WEDNESDAY, 6TH OCTOBER
Sun trine Uranus

Your emotions will be stirred up in an unusual manner today. You may fall head over heels in love with an unusually attractive personality. Any such attraction would be sudden, electric and quite devastating; however, it may not stand the test of time. Indeed, it may have gone off the boil by the end of the day and, instead of being whisked off to someone's boudoir, you could finish up in bed with a good book and a cup of cocoa!

GEMINI

THURSDAY, 7TH OCTOBER
Venus into Virgo

Old scores and family squabbles can now be laid to rest as the passage of Venus into your domestic area signals a time of harmony and contentment. Surround yourself with beauty, both in terms of affection and in material possessions. This is a good time to renew a closeness with those you love. Join forces to complete a major project such as redecoration, or even a move of home itself. Be assured that the stars smile on you now.

FRIDAY, 8TH OCTOBER
Moon trine Neptune

You won't have to please anyone apart from yourself today. This is a time to indulge your more refined tastes by listening to music, go dancing or enjoy a good film.

SATURDAY, 9TH OCTOBER
New Moon

There's a New Moon today casting a glow over your artistic potential. Your talents should shine now so have some belief in yourself and in what you can offer to the world at large. Of course if art and literature leave you cold, you may be more inclined to an amorous path. Conventional values are not for you now since you're determined to be yourself and to chart your own course. Make time to have fun, you deserve it.

SUNDAY, 10TH OCTOBER
Venus trine Jupiter

The strong influence of Venus shows the need to improve your personal environment. Get some plants in, throw some colourful cushions about and generally create an atmosphere of the exotic in your home. Once done, you'll feel like a million dollars!

MONDAY, 11TH OCTOBER
Jupiter square Neptune

Your sense of reality seems to take a break today landing you in the middle of other people's fantasies. Though there are times when this might be an enjoyable experience – this is not one of them! Steer clear of those who would lead you astray!

TUESDAY, 12TH OCTOBER
Void Moon

This is not a great day in which to decide anything or to start anything new. A void Moon suggests that there are no major planetary aspects being made, either between planets or involving the Sun or the Moon. This is a fairly unusual situation but it does happen from time to time and the only way to deal with it is to stick to your usual routines and do nothing special for a while.

WEDNESDAY, 13TH OCTOBER
Mercury square Uranus

Your restlessness and boredom could have far-reaching consequences today. If your job is too tedious, you're likely just to walk out and do something far more interesting. If that's the case, I just hope that your job will still be there when you decide to return.

THURSDAY, 14TH OCTOBER
Neptune direct

The planet Neptune moves into direct motion today and this will bring a recent period of uncertainty to an end. Many of you have loved ones living at a distance from you and, over the past few months, you may have felt unable to help them deal with their problems because of the distance. You, or a member of your family, may also have been in a dilemma about religious or philosophical matters.

FRIDAY, 15TH OCTOBER
Moon conjunct Mars

Something important concerning relationships must be tackled over the next few weeks. You and your lover will be putting extra energy into your relationship now. This may be in the form of taking up a sporting hobby or some other kind of shared interest now or you may simply decide to see a bit more of each other. Business or working partnerships will benefit from this planetary movement too.

SATURDAY, 16TH OCTOBER
Mercury opposite Saturn

It seems you have a mental block today. No matter how hard you try you can't get to grips with a problem. The trouble is that Mercury's opposition to Saturn has clouded your thinking processes. The solution might be right under your nose but you can't see it. Have some patience, the clouds will clear.

SUNDAY, 17TH OCTOBER
Mars into Capricorn

Mars moves into your Solar eighth house today, raising the level of your feelings to some kind of fever pitch. Your passions will be aroused in some important way

GEMINI

and you could find yourself behaving in an unusual manner due to the depth of your emotions. Make sure that you are not simply reacting out of anger or out of some kind of feverish response to anything today.

MONDAY, 18TH OCTOBER
Venus square Pluto

A home-based project or a desire you have to make a new and rather expensive purchase for your home will not find favour with your other half today. If you don't want to cause fireworks, the pair of you had better agree to disagree on this topic!

TUESDAY, 19TH OCTOBER
Moon square Saturn

You are no stranger to hard work, and as long as you feel as though this is worthwhile you can take pride in a job well done. However, today's stars hint at a waste of time and effort so think your tasks through before you start.

WEDNESDAY, 20TH OCTOBER
Moon sextile Jupiter

If you play your cards right, and by that we mean close to your chest, today could provide an excellent opportunity in the workplace. A confidence must be kept and a secret could do your worldly fortunes a lot of good.

THURSDAY, 21ST OCTOBER
Moon opposite Venus

Your life needs some kind of alteration or rearranging now. You may have too many burdens being placed upon you at the moment both at home and at work and you will need to sort these out soon before they break your back in two. You may need more help from those around you or you may have to take on some kind of staff to do some of your jobs for you.

FRIDAY, 22ND OCTOBER
Sun square Neptune

You may long for freedom today, only to find yourself bound by chores, duties and obligations. However someone close to you or friendly to you will help you to get these done as quickly as possible so that you can escape from the drudgery for a while at least. There may be unexpected help with a legal or an official matter of some kind today and it should be a youngish man who comes up with this.

GEMINI

SATURDAY, 23RD OCTOBER
Sun into Scorpio

The Sun moves into your Solar sixth house of work and duty for the next month. This Solar movement will also encourage you to concentrate on your health and well-being and also that of your family. If you are off-colour, the Sun will help you to get back to full health once again. If you have jobs that need to be done, the next month or so will be a good time to get them done.

SUNDAY, 24TH OCTOBER
Full Moon

Apart from a slightly frustrating Full Moon situation today, there is not much going on in the planetary firmament. The best thing to do is to stick to your usual way of doing things and to avoid starting anything new or important. If you feel off-colour or out of sorts, then take whatever medicines you need and try not to work too hard.

MONDAY, 25TH OCTOBER
Venus trine Saturn

A period of time spent with an older member of your family will be emotionally fulfilling to both of you. A sense of parental guidance is evident today and you'll be thankful for it. A sober sense of reality will help you make sense of your own family situation.

TUESDAY, 26TH OCTOBER
Moon opposite Mercury

If you are engaged in a long and detailed task such as dressmaking, do-it-yourself or craftwork of some other kind, you may find the going difficult today. You may encounter unexpected difficulties in your task or you may have to set the whole job aside in order to do something more important for a while. Work of all kinds could be frustrating for at least part of the day today.

WEDNESDAY, 27TH OCTOBER
Moon opposite Pluto

You will find it hard to work out what is going on in the minds of those nearest to you and, worse still, they will also find it very hard to understand your motives. This lack of mutual understanding may lead to a disagreement over money matters or of something more important and much more subtle, such as when to begin a particular course of action or what road to take.

GEMINI

THURSDAY, 28TH OCTOBER
Mercury sextile Neptune

A chat to a loved one will confirm that you are on the right track. New faces coming into your life will have a beneficial effect on you and your future in many different ways.

FRIDAY, 29TH OCTOBER
Moon opposite Mars

Financial worries govern the day as the Moon opposes Mars in fiscal areas of your chart. Try not to over-react to any minor economic problems. Your temper is frayed but if you are systematic you can sort out monetary problems before they arise.

SATURDAY, 30TH OCTOBER
Mercury into Sagittarius

The inquisitive Mercury moves into your Solar house of marriage and long-lasting relationships from today ushering in a period when a renewed understanding can be reached between yourself and your partner. New relationships, too, can be formed under this influence though these will tend to be on a light, fairly superficial level. Good humour and plenty of charm should be a feature for a few weeks, though you must try to curb a tendency to needlessly criticize another's foibles. Remember, not even you are perfect!

SUNDAY, 31ST OCTOBER
Moon square Sun

It wouldn't be a good idea to overload your schedule too much today. We know that you're bounding with self-confidence but the vitality levels just aren't up to it at the moment. If you're working, the evening won't come around fast enough. If not, then leave domestic chores for now. A few unwashed dishes aren't the end of the world.

November at a Glance

LOVE	♥	♥	♥	♥	
WORK	★	★	★		
MONEY	£	£	£	£	£
HEALTH	✪	✪	✪	✪	✪
LUCK	⊌	⊌	⊌	⊌	

MONDAY, 1ST NOVEMBER
Void Moon

Today is one of those odd days when there are no important planetary aspects being made, not even to the Moon. The best way to tackle these kinds of days is to stick to your usual routine and to avoid starting anything new or tackling anything of major importance. If you do decide to do something large today, then it will take longer and be harder to cope with than it would normally.

TUESDAY, 2ND NOVEMBER
Moon square Mercury

No sooner does Mercury open channels of communication, you're back into a cycle of misunderstanding and mistrust. Perhaps you aren't putting in enough effort in the clarity of speech that you should. Take it slowly, wounds don't heal in ten minutes, so it's still important to gently renew the trust.

WEDNESDAY, 3RD NOVEMBER
Moon trine Saturn

Visits from your parents or other family members will bring you joy and happiness now. All your family relationships will be calm and pleasant for the time being.

THURSDAY, 4TH NOVEMBER
Moon sextile Mercury

It's time for fun and togetherness as the Moon and Mercury highlight romantic potentials and partnerships. Forget mundane worries and get out with the sole aim of enjoying yourself. The presence of someone special makes this a time to remember.

GEMINI

FRIDAY, 5TH NOVEMBER
Moon trine Uranus

You could be swept off your feet by a sudden attraction today and, if so, you may never be quite the same again. If it is love that carries you away today, the chances are that the object of your affection is a foreigner or someone from a culture and background which is very different from your own. You may suddenly realize that you feel more for a friend than you first thought.

SATURDAY, 6TH NOVEMBER
Sun opposite Saturn

This is one of those days when it would be too easy to look on the black side of things. Remember that though you may think that the world is full of gloom and doom, every cloud does have a silver lining. All you have to do is find it. Cheer up!

SUNDAY, 7TH NOVEMBER
Sun sextile Mars

There's a golden opportunity to improve your financial status today. The Sun and Mars are well aspected showing that you can increase your savings or make an advantageous investment. It would be a good time to resolve some old debts, and to make some regular contributions to a pension fund or other long-term scheme. Your sure instincts won't let you down now.

MONDAY, 8TH NOVEMBER
New Moon

Today's New Moon gives you the stamina to shrug off any minor ailments that have been troubling you. Occurring, as it does, in your Solar house of health and work, it's obvious that you need to get yourself into shape to face the challenges that await you. A few early nights, a better diet and a readiness to give up bad habits such as smoking, will work wonders.

TUESDAY, 9TH NOVEMBER
Mercury into Scorpio

Some monetary worries should be alleviated by Mercury's change of sign today. Of course, this does not come without effort and you may find that you have to take on a part-time job in the short term to get the books to balance. More generally, improvements in the job stakes are now possible, but you'll have to be keenly aware of the possible competition and prepared to act instantly to get the employment you want.

GEMINI

WEDNESDAY, 10TH NOVEMBER
Moon sextile Uranus

A loved one could surprise you with an exotic meal or a night out at some romantic spot. Don't even think about putting up any resistance! Just go with the flow and forget mundane cares for a while.

THURSDAY, 11TH NOVEMBER
Moon trine Jupiter

Put on your dancing shoes, grab your partner and head for the high life tonight. Whatever you do and wherever you go, you are set to become the social sensation of the year. If you are single, then get out and about and see who else is alone and available. If you are married, then look to the future and discuss shared aims and intentions with your partner.

FRIDAY, 12TH NOVEMBER
Moon square Venus

You and your lover seem to be sorting out some of your problems now and this is definitely the time to kiss and make up. Fortunately for you, the making up is likely to lead to an outburst of sheer passion, so make the most of each other's company while your libidos are so in tune. You may be asked to invest in a glamorous scheme and, although this looks like a dodgy idea, it may be worth taking a small chance.

SATURDAY, 13TH NOVEMBER
Moon conjunct Mars

Restraint is the key to personal success as the Moon conjuncts Mars in one of the most intimate areas of your chart. You may be tempted to use sexual allure to get your own way, or you may find yourself the victim of emotional blackmail. An authority figure could get above himself or you'll find that partnership funds are seriously depleted. Keep a sense of perspective.

SUNDAY, 14TH NOVEMBER
Saturn square Uranus

Old habits die hard they say, and that's certainly true today, even when you'd just love to sweep them all away in one go and start all over again. There's a mighty tussle going on between Uranus and Saturn, or to put it another way, between the new and the old. You'll have to decide which one eventually!

GEMINI

MONDAY, 15TH NOVEMBER
Moon square Saturn

This is likely to be one of those days when you are restless, yet your get-up-and-go has got up and gone! Whatever you do today, you'll want to be doing something else.

TUESDAY, 16TH NOVEMBER
Mercury sextile Mars

You're a shrewd operator today. Complex financial affairs can't get the better of you. Neither can officialdom nor red tape. You've got the measure of all opposition and have the brain and the brawn to deal with all of it!

WEDNESDAY, 17TH NOVEMBER
Venus sextile Pluto

I hope that your energy levels are on a high because the passionate intensity revealed by today's stars shows that physical action is a probability. The combination of loving Venus and intense Pluto spells a session of steamy sensuality.

THURSDAY, 18TH NOVEMBER
Moon trine Mercury

If you have been feeling frustrated and unable to get any sense out of anybody, today's excellent aspect between the Moon and Mercury will sweep all that away. You will be able to make great strides at work, or in any kind of setting where an appreciation of your status and authority make the wheels turn smoothly.

FRIDAY, 19TH NOVEMBER
Moon sextile Neptune

A trip to the theatre or cinema in the company of good friends is on offer today. Forget duty for once and have some fun. You have been under stress recently and could do with a light-hearted break.

SATURDAY, 20TH NOVEMBER
Venus trine Uranus

You will be full of bright ideas which will, fortunately, turn out to be quite practical when you put them to the test. A woman friend or relative will surprise you by taking you out to see or do something interesting. You may enjoy a mild but quite disturbing flirtation today, and this could have the effect of making you feel restless and uncertain about your usual partnerships or relationships.

GEMINI

SUNDAY, 21ST NOVEMBER
Mars square Jupiter

There could be some kind of unexpected expense which hits you and your partner at the same time. There is no use arguing about this, just get together and pay the darned thing, even if it means that you are both a bit short of the 'readies' for the rest of the month. If you feel really fed up with a particular person or a particular situation now, do something to change things today.

MONDAY, 22ND NOVEMBER
Sun into Sagittarius

The Sun moves into the area of your chart devoted to relationships from today. If things have been difficult in a partnership, either personal or in business, then this is your chance to put everything back into its proper place. It's obvious that the significant other in your life deserves respect and affection and that's just what you're now prepared to give. Teamwork is the key to success over the next month.

TUESDAY, 23RD NOVEMBER
Full Moon

The Full Moon in your sign shows that you've come to the end of a personal phase and that it's time to tie up the loose ends and move on. This should be an opportunity to rid yourself of harmful little habits and create a whole new persona. This could be an image transformation. So, if you're at all dissatisfied by the way you present yourself to the world, then work out your own personal make-over. You'll be astounded by the reception the new you gets.

WEDNESDAY, 24TH NOVEMBER
Moon trine Venus

The love life receives a welcome boost today as the Moon and Venus conspire to fire up passionate intensity. Being a creature of impulse, you shouldn't find it too much of a problem to arrange an evening of amorous dalliance. A trip to the theatre or cinema would bring a little sparkle into your relationship.

THURSDAY, 25TH NOVEMBER
Sun sextile Neptune

You are likely to be with someone today who affects your heart quite profoundly. The influence of this other person may introduce you to psychic or spiritual matters and this may lead you to investigate something like astrology, divination or spiritual healing. You may visit a medium or you may have a strange, out-of-the-body type of experience yourself.

GEMINI

FRIDAY, 26TH NOVEMBER
Mars into Aquarius

You could find yourself travelling over great distances at some time during the next few weeks. You may be asked to visit friends or family who live overseas now or you may simply take advantage of a good holiday offer. You may restrict your travelling to mental journeys by taking up a course of study or training now.

SATURDAY, 27TH NOVEMBER
Moon opposite Neptune

You may begin to doubt your own sanity at times today, you will certainly doubt your own judgement and, to some extent, your doubts may be justified. Neptune will bring muddle and misunderstandings all around you and all your normal lines of communication will break down or will cease to make sense for a while. Someone may run you down behind your back or you may be unjustly accused of something.

SUNDAY, 28TH NOVEMBER
Moon square Mercury

It's a very tense outlook today for the Moon and Mercury put your nerves on edge. Of course, your own anxieties will prove to be far more exhausting than any outside influence in your life just now. If you're wise, you'll avoid challenges today and indulge in some relaxation. If you do insist on facing up to every little thing that the world throws at you, you'll end up depleted and glum.

MONDAY, 29TH NOVEMBER
Mars conjunct Neptune

You will be called on to help others now and you will go to this task with a will. You may do something charitable in an organized kind of way, such as helping out at a local hospital or being involved in an entertainment for handicapped or sick people. This is also a good time to think about travel and to make plans for your future holidays, so get the brochures out and dream a little.

TUESDAY, 30TH NOVEMBER
Moon trine Saturn

A bit of peace and quiet is all you need to put you back on an even keel. Some time spent alone in the comfort of your own home will sort you out mentally and emotionally. Don't be persuaded to socialize against your better judgement.

December at a Glance

LOVE	❤				
WORK	★	★	★	★	★
MONEY	£	£			
HEALTH	✛	✛	✛	✛	
LUCK	♘	♘	♘	♘	

WEDNESDAY, 1ST DECEMBER
Venus opposite Jupiter

The heart rules the head in no uncertain manner today. Venus and Jupiter are in opposition so common sense has flown. Your heart is worn on your sleeve and you are heading for some hurt if you aren't careful. It's difficult to keep a sense of perspective when everyone around you, even your closest friends, encourage a romantic folly.

THURSDAY, 2ND DECEMBER
Moon sextile Sun

Love is on your agenda today so, whether you are in the throes of a fresh and new love affair or whether you are happily settled in a relationship of long standing, all dealings with your other half will make you happy now.

FRIDAY, 3RD DECEMBER
Moon opposite Jupiter

Children could cost you money now or they could in some way prevent you from taking up an appealing offer or two. You may be restricted by obligations to your family and you will have to put duty and responsibilities before personal freedom for a while. It is worth letting your friends know how much you value them because they do help to lift your spirits when they can.

SATURDAY, 4TH DECEMBER
Moon square Neptune

Try not to take anything on face value today. Messages could be garbled and friends will get the wrong end of the stick. Watch out for someone who is trying to pull the wool over your eyes.

GEMINI

SUNDAY, 5TH DECEMBER
Venus into Scorpio

Venus moves out of the fun, sun and pleasure area of your chart into the work, duty and health area, and it will stay there for the next few weeks. This suggests that any problems related to work and duty will become easier to handle and also that you could start to see some kind of practical outcome from all that you have been doing lately. If you have been off-colour recently, Venus will help you to feel better soon.

MONDAY, 6TH DECEMBER
Sun sextile Uranus

You could fall in love with an attractive and fascinating stranger today! Even if you don't actually go this far, you will certainly be attracted to someone new and you will probably be equally attractive to them in turn. Enjoy this flirtatious mood for what it is and be careful not to allow yourself to get into trouble – unless you want to, of course. You may be restless and in need of freedom today.

TUESDAY, 7TH DECEMBER
New Moon

The only planetary activity today is a New Moon in your opposite sign. It is possible that this could bring the start of a new relationship for the lonely but, to be honest, this planetary aspect is a bit too weak for such a big event. It is much more likely that you will improve on a current relationship rather than start a new one at this time.

WEDNESDAY, 8TH DECEMBER
Venus square Neptune

There are times when letting your heart rule your head is not a good idea. Today's harsh aspect between Venus and Neptune doesn't do much for your common sense so keep your tongue in your cheek when attractive travel or work ventures are discussed. It's likely that they're nothing more than hot air!

THURSDAY, 9TH DECEMBER
Moon sextile Venus

What a romantic and loving day this is. However, you are in such a soppy mood that you may find yourself agreeing to do something for your lover that, under other, more sober circumstances, you would never have agreed to at all.

FRIDAY, 10TH DECEMBER
Mars square Saturn

When Mars and Saturn are in such a hard aspect it's not going to be an easy day! This is not a good time for travelling, taking exams or attending interviews. You could be too impatient for your own good and make silly mistakes. Take care.

SATURDAY, 11TH DECEMBER
Mercury into Sagittarius

Mercury moves into the area of your chart which is concerned with relationships that are open and above board now. This suggests that over the next few weeks you will have nothing to be secretive about in connection with your relationships with others. Your friendships will be free and easy and your lovers the kind whom you can happily take home to mother!

SUNDAY, 12TH DECEMBER
Mercury sextile Neptune

There's a soft, dreamy and pretty romantic aura surrounding you today. It sounds like a recipe for candlelight and an intimate tête-à-tête with someone you love.

MONDAY, 13TH DECEMBER
Moon sextile Sun

You have a longing for far-off, exotic places but going on your own won't be much fun. You need someone around you to share an adventure now. However, if you are on your own, go anyway. You'll find someone to be with when you get to wherever you're going!

TUESDAY, 14TH DECEMBER
Mars conjunct Uranus

You'll be fiercely intellectual today, able to eloquently argue you point and reduce anyone foolish enough to stand against you to rubble! Travel may be a feature, but if that's the case take care because the planets are particularly disruptive today!

WEDNESDAY, 15TH DECEMBER
Venus opposite Saturn

The ill-will of a rival will become very clear today. Though you may have done nothing to deserve such spite, you could still be wounded be this attitude. Rise above such pettiness and don't dignify remarks with any reaction at all.

GEMINI

THURSDAY, 16TH DECEMBER
Moon sextile Neptune

An outing with friends will be very enjoyable today. In fact, the atmosphere will be so convivial that even if you're on your own, you won't remain in that state for long since new friends will find you!

FRIDAY, 17TH DECEMBER
Sun trine Jupiter

Never mind the expense, romance is more important! Take the one who means most to you out for a night on the town. This is a supremely lucky day for you to have a lot of fun and to bask in affection. Your lover will appreciate the treat.

SATURDAY, 18TH DECEMBER
Mercury conjunct Pluto

You (or your partner) will have a bee in your bonnet and will get no peace until you have told somebody. If this obsessive attitude is a problem then it's about time it came out into the open in any case. This could indicate a clearing of the air.

SUNDAY, 19TH DECEMBER
Moon conjunct Saturn

Peace and quiet is all that you will crave today. You may have something to do that requires a fair amount of concentration so the last thing that you'll want is interruptions. Take the phone off the hook and pretend to be out while you get on with it.

MONDAY, 20TH DECEMBER
Jupiter into Aries

The movement of Jupiter into the most social area of your chart shows that your taste for fun and good companionship will grow stronger over the coming year. Good friends will be worth their weight in gold, because they will advise you and support you through thick and thin.

TUESDAY, 21ST DECEMBER
Moon opposite Pluto

The thorny problems of dealing with others raises its head again today. You may have to change your ideas radically or, better still, work out which of your ideas is worth keeping and which is really just a matter of hanging on to outworn prejudices. All this soul-searching will be necessary if you are going to make your relations with others work smoothly in the future. You may need to change someone else's mind too.

GEMINI

WEDNESDAY, 22ND DECEMBER
Sun into Capricorn

Today, the Sun enters your Solar eighth house of beginnings and endings. Thus, over the next month, you can expect something to wind its way to a conclusion, while something else starts to take its place. This doesn't seem to signify a major turning point or any really big event in your life but it does mark one of those small turning points that we all go through from time to time.

THURSDAY, 23RD DECEMBER
Full Moon

If you've been sensible with your cash, today's Full Moon shows that there are certain monetary strictures that may no longer be needed. Areas in which you've been lax need attention too, for spendthrift tendencies may require corrective measures. This is a time to sort out your fiscal state for the greatest advantage. Like a plant, some judicious pruning and encouraging would do your bank balance a lot of good.

FRIDAY, 24TH DECEMBER
Venus square Mars

It may be Christmas Eve but the daily habits of life seem all too restricting and limited at the moment and you'll be looking for something to alleviate your boredom. You know that there's more to life than the usual grind and will be anxious for new experience and stimulation. It's unfortunate that your self-expression suffers from this mood so try not to be too negative or sarcastic to those around you.

SATURDAY, 25TH DECEMBER
Moon trine Pluto

You and your partner should have no difficulty in communicating with each other on this Christmas day. You may be able to clear the air or to get a better idea of what your other half has in mind. There could be good news in connection with joint financial matters and it is possible that your partner could be doing better than expected by now.

SUNDAY, 26TH DECEMBER
Mercury sextile Mars

If you are in a settled relationship such as marriage, you should try suggesting to your partner that you take a trip or holiday soon; he or she will probably jump at the chance. If you are single, then get yourself involved in any kind or outdoorsy hobby which brings you into contact with interesting people.

GEMINI

MONDAY, 27TH DECEMBER
Mercury trine Jupiter

Those two merry planets Jupiter and Mercury combine to make you quite merry as well – in both senses of the word. Parties and get-togethers of all kinds will be the perfect arena for you to give a display of your wit and repartee.

TUESDAY, 28TH DECEMBER
Moon square Mercury

Just when you want a quiet and restful day, other people will have quite different ideas. You may have to get down to some do-it-yourself jobs in or around the house and, just when you thought you had finished and could look forward to sitting down and reading the paper for a while, your ever-loving partner will come up with yet more jobs for you to do.

WEDNESDAY, 29TH DECEMBER
Moon square Sun

Isn't it time you took a good look at the state of your savings? We know that all you want to do is have fun now, but casting an eye over your bank statement would be sensible. You may find that you've pushed the boat out a little too far for comfort and it's time you started putting some cash back into your emergency funds. Think about saving for a rainy day. You know it makes sense.

THURSDAY, 30TH DECEMBER
Mars sextile Jupiter

The pursuit of happiness is all very well but you need to develop a little wisdom and understanding along the way. Therefore, you could now find yourself thinking over important matters and also taking the trouble to find something out before making any major decisions. You could start a course of training today or you may decide to take lessons which would help you improve at your chosen sport or hobby.

FRIDAY, 31ST DECEMBER
Venus into Sagittarius

Venus, the planet of romance, moves into your horoscope area of close relationships on the last day of the year, increasing your physical desires and bringing the light of love into your heart. If you're involved in a long-term partnership it's a chance to renew the magic of the early days of your union. If single, then the next few weeks should bring a stunning new attraction into your life. Happy New Century!